BARRY DANIELS was [...]
worked in the USA as a singer [...]
returning to the UK where he married Carmen.
They have two children, Charly and Rhys. In 1992
they discovered that both children were suffering
from Batten's disease. Having fought the government
for the right to save Rhys with a ground-breaking
bone marrow transplant, Barry set up The Daniels
Charitable Trust, a national charity to help other sick
children and their families.

TERRY MANNERS is Assistant Editor of the *Daily Express*.
He was formerly Night Editor of the newspaper for
five years, a period spanning big stories such as the
Gulf War, the fall of Prime Minister Margaret
Thatcher and the Yeltsin Revolution.

He has written five books, is a barker for the Variety
Club of Great Britain and a member of the Press
Association's panel of advisory editors. He lives with
his family on the Essex coast.

Rhys
The Fight
for Life

Barry Daniels with Terry Manners

Virgin

First published in Great Britain in 1995 by
Virgin Books
an imprint of Virgin Publishing Ltd
332 Ladbroke Grove
London W10 5AH

A catalogue record for this book is available from the
British Library

ISBN 0 86369 983 9

Typeset by Galleon Typesetting
Printed and bound in Great Britain
by BPC Paperbacks Ltd

Contents

Contents

Acknowledgements

We would like to show our extreme appreciation to Professor John Hobbs for his vision and words of encouragement, Dr Ashok Vellodi for his support and friendship, Alan Meyer for his great support and concern for the family and Mr Al Fayed for his utmost concern for Charly & Rhys.

A special thank you to all at The Bristol Royal Hospital for Sick Children, Dr Tony Oakhill, Jackie Cornish, Colin Steward, Dawn Payter and the rest of the wonderful people who work there.

Also Bill and Suzanne Wyman for showing us such friendship; Lorraine and the wonderful crew at Sticky Fingers; and to a great friend, Penny Thompson, lots of love. To all the people around the world who have been affected by this devastating disease: we fight this battle together!

Illustrations

Rhys makes friends with a horse in Epping Forest the day before he leaves home for his second bone marrow transplant

Charly and Rhys with Fred Flintstone in Universal Studios, Florida, in March 1993

Charly snuggles down in her lovely new beanbag

17 June 1993. Rhys salutes the hordes of waiting cameramen (*Guardian*)

Rhys fights his way back to health after his second transplant in September 1994

1: One Last Chance

'I'm sorry, would you mind explaining that again?' asked Barry.

He and Carmen were shattered. They sat in the little white-walled, hospital room staring at the consultant, not wanting to believe what they were being told. How much bad luck could one couple have? Why them?

'I'm sorry but the scans have revealed that your little boy's brainwaves are severely abnormal,' said Dr Tony Oakhill. His words confirmed their worst fears – the onset of the rare illness that was already killing their beautiful, six-year-old daughter Charly. Now their son Rhys, aged just three, could be developing Batten's disease too.

'It means the new transplant on Friday is now even more important in our race against time to save your little boy before his condition deteriorates further,' Dr Oakhill added, nervously flicking through his notes. Barry could tell he didn't like giving bad news even though he must have had enough practice.

'It will be around a hundred days before we know if the new bone marrow has any chance of curing Rhys.'

Barry put his arm around Carmen and they walked slowly back to the little sealed unit that Rhys was living in along the corridor at Bristol's Royal Hospital for Sick Children.

Carmen was so tired she almost couldn't make it to the room. Barry half carried her and she smiled gratefully at him. He was tired too, tired of hearing bad news.

Some drugs were being pumped through a tube directly into their son's blood stream. Others he swallowed daily. The cocktail of eight different medicines was preparing him for his second, history-making bone marrow transplant in a few days' time.

The plucky little fighter was already the only Batten's disease victim in the world to have had such a transplant. Barry and Carmen were clutching at straws. They had learned in Germany that experimental bone marrow transplants had been performed on dogs with similar conditions. It had been their decision to volunteer their precious son for such experimental surgery. The question was, would it work on a human? Some people, doctors included, had been against it but Barry and Carmen were prepared to take the risk. The alternative was too depressing to contemplate.

The aim of the transplant was to restore a missing enzyme in the brain capable of breaking down a build-up of cell-destroying protein that would eventually lead to vastly accelerated dementia not normally experienced until old age. But Rhys's first transplant had failed.

The new surgery was his last chance and at this moment his immune system was at such a low ebb that the slightest exposure to any form of germ could trigger a relapse. If the new transplant failed too, he would probably die within five years.

The couple looked down at Rhys in the isolation cubicle. They desperately wanted to pick up their son's little hand and kiss his fingers. He was part of their very souls and their hearts and their lives. And they knew he always would be, no matter what.

Carmen could hardly watch when a nurse came to insert a needle in her son's arm. She smiled down at him, an assurance that everything would be OK. He looked up trusting her, but she felt the tears come traitorously out to her eyelashes. She made her eyes wider and wider, trying to keep the drops from falling down her cheeks so he would not see them. Yet another needle, yet another cocktail of drugs. Rhys hadn't ordered it: they had ordered it for Rhys. They were inflicting pain and distress on their son. They prayed that one day he would be able to thank them for it.

Barry and Carmen knew it was only a matter of time before he developed clinical symptoms of Batten's disease, a neurological disorder which affects one in 30,000 children in Britain and usually kills by the age of eight. First diagnosed in 1903 by British surgeon Dr Batten, founder of paediatric neurology in Britain, the disease has a more formidable name – neuronal ceroid lipofuscinosis. Technically, it means an accumulation of fatty pigments in the cells of the brain that affect the nervous system. Missing enzymes in the body's chemistry leave the victims unable to break down such fats and their associated sugars and proteins.

Rhys's sister Charly was so ill with the condition that she was back in nappies, had to be spoonfed and was almost blind.

For the last two weeks Rhys had undergone intensive chemotherapy in preparation for his operation.

3

The chemotherapy had destroyed his own natural immune system making his body ready to receive the new bone marrow – but it meant that the slightest infection could be fatal.

Marrow was being collected from the donor, a woman, under general anaesthetic in a few days' time. The bone marrow cells were to be taken with a syringe from the cavity at the base of her back. No operation was involved. The transplant would be given to Rhys like a blood transfusion through a Hickman line into his chest rather than his arm. It would feed straight into his blood stream.

'Why don't you go home, love? There's nothing else you can do,' said Barry. Carmen quietly poured two cups of tea from the pot on the little brown table by the window in Rhys's room and without a word stood watching her son drift off to sleep. She was angry inside now that fate seemed to be taking so much from them.

'Yes,' she said after a while, 'I'll go home to Charly.'

A worldwide appeal sponsored by the *Daily Express* in London had found the bone marrow donor – the one person in 40,000 who had any chance of saving Rhys's life. The search for a donor had been difficult because Rhys had a rare tissue type and at one stage Barry thought they would never find the right person. Now they had. At least something was going right in their lives.

Barry and Carmen knew what lay ahead if the transplant failed. They faced the prospect of feeding Rhys through a tube within a few years. They had already spent months watching his every move to see if he showed any signs of the clinical symptoms that had beset his elder sister.

They watched for him to trip up or stumble or slur his words. If and when that happened they knew they would be too late. At that point they would end up burying both their children before the age of ten. Barry put the thought out of his mind, but it kept creeping in again as he made himself busy tidying up the little room, pinning cards from wellwishers to the wall and lining up the teddy bears and Action Men dolls like soldiers on a parade ground.

He stopped for a moment and looked down into the isolation cubicle at Rhys who had opened his sleepy eyes again.

'Where's Charly, daddy? I want to see Charly,' he mumbled, the drugs now wrapping his mind into a ball of cotton wool.

Barry wanted to pick Rhys up and take him away. He sometimes had second thoughts about putting his son through all this pain – and he had them now.

How different life had been a few years earlier.

They were all as close then as they were now. But then they laughed and talked and cried and hugged and joked together. Now there weren't any jokes or hugs or laughs or talks. Only tears.

The flowers and the trees were all in bloom when Carmen arrived home in the August sunshine. Somehow she expected it all to look different, like her own life. But it looked the same, as if nothing was wrong with the world. It was as if she was living in another time, looking down on everything going on below her.

After hugging Charly and waving farewell to Barry's cousin Julie who had been looking after her while Carmen was at the hospital in Bristol, she stood for a minute, looking at herself in the mirror in the hall. She felt old. She felt she looked old. She felt she had failed. She closed her eyes for a moment remembering how she and Barry had met at the family wedding anniversary party.

She had been a barmaid of eighteen and he a 27-year-old project manager for a record and video distribution company. The following year they had moved in together. Then she became pregnant with Charly and they had married. Funny, all that time could be summed up in just a few thoughts. Perhaps one day she would look back on the nightmare she was living now and it would all be summed up in a few dreamlike memories.

Carmen looked across the hall into the lounge where Charly was lying on the sofa, her big blue eyes staring at the ceiling. She was so gorgeous that at the age of two she had modelled for the children's chain Trotters and had auditioned for a contract with Peaudouce nappies. They had only stopped going to the auditions because Charly had seemed somehow flustered and had kept bumping into things. They believed the stress of it all was getting to her. But it wasn't really the stress at all. It was something else, something they couldn't possibly have known about.

Their world should have been complete when they had Rhys. 'But then came the beginning of the end of our world,' Carmen said quietly to herself.

The mental images of how Barry had found Charly slumped motionless in a chair with her eyes open flashed through her mind. And the doctor, the doctor who had diagnosed Charly as epileptic and prescribed the drugs which made her condition worse. And the tests at Great Ormond Street Hospital, the heartbreaking moment they sat in front of the consultant and heard those strange words, 'Batten's disease'.

'Batten's disease.' Carmen said the words out loud and found herself looking out of her bedroom window. She didn't know how she got there, she didn't even remember walking up the stairs. She stared across the road at the birthday cards lined up on her neighbour's window-sill. God, how she hated birthdays . . . and Christmas . . . and Mother's Day.

Suddenly, she found herself holding Charly's christening shawl. She had taken it down from the top shelf of the wardrobe but she didn't know why. She remembered the church, the service, the family and friends standing quietly around the font. The shawl seemed a relic of a lost life, of a moment in time when everything was different, a moment that was lost for ever. She folded it carefully and put it back on the shelf. She didn't really know what to do with it, but in a way it seemed like it was all she had left to remind her of happier times.

Barry was still in Bristol with Rhys and she would be joining them again later that week. But for her the next few days before Rhys's second transplant seemed to drag by like a rainy day that never ends. She looked after Charly, washing her and brushing her hair and talking to her and rubbing her little feet and telling herself that her son's transplant had to work, it just had to.

Barry picked up the bleeping mobile telephone and answered the reporter's questions.

'Yes, we rely on the doctors. If they thought the transplant was pointless, they would obviously advise against it . . . Yes, all our hopes are pinned on Friday evening when our son will be fighting for his life . . . Yes, we live for our children. We would do anything for them . . . Yes, Carmen as a mother is

7

feeling a lot more pain than me. She is tied up with the kids every minute of every hour of every day of the year. No . . . that's it. Rhys is waking up. He needs me. No, I can't let you in for a picture.'

He quietly put down the receiver wanting to be alone with his thoughts. If only the press knew about the rows and the tears. What he and Carmen were really going through. He wondered how a reporter would handle it, if it happened to him or her. True, they seemed kind and concerned, but they were just doing their jobs, then going to the pub or home to the kids, or planning a weekend in the country, or thinking about their next bonk. What if they were suddenly confronted with the news that their children had an incurable disease, how would they handle the reporters at their door? In his heart Barry knew they just had no idea about the strain on his relationship with Carmen, how he snapped when he didn't mean to, had full-scale rows about stupid, meaningless things like there being no butter in the house or no milk for a cup of tea. How sometimes he and Carmen could hardly bring themselves to speak to each other and yet put on an act for neighbours, family and journalists. No one had any real idea of what was going on indoors. The sobbing and the heartbreak. The shouting and the despair. The jokes that really didn't come off but they both laughed at.

He remembered Britain's best-known transplant patient, little Laura Davis, and her parents. Fran and Les Davis split up just a few months after Laura's death. Barry and Carmen had seen Batten's disease take a similar toll on other relationships. Some people just couldn't take the strain. They felt guilty and blamed themselves because the illness was genetic.

Barry and Carmen didn't know whether the disease

8

had been in their families for hundreds of years or, as Dr Baritzer of Great Ormond Street had told them, if it was just a mismatch of chromosomes at conception for both of them. When both parents carry the Batten's gene, they have a 25 per cent chance of producing a child with the disease and a 50 per cent chance of having a child who is also a carrier. But no tests are available to determine carriers. What they did know was that it was just no good dwelling on what had happened. That wouldn't help or solve anything.

What was the use of blaming themselves or anyone else? It was here. As real as the sunlight but not as welcome. They knew they just had to live with it, like so many other things in their lives – so they just got on with it, and they would see it through until the bitter end. Yes, it was a strain on Barry's relationship with Carmen and Carmen's relationship with Barry. Yes, it was hard finding time to talk. They would go two months without ever stepping out of the front door, just the two of them.

The daylight was fading as Barry drew the brightly coloured curtains in Rhys's room. God, how he hated the dark. Somehow, when the night came he felt worse. Hopefully, Rhys would sleep through and then he too could sleep the darkness away. He was tired. He needed some rest to recharge his batteries for the next day's fight. The battle was just beginning again. As he sat for a moment staring at the ceiling he knew the fight was going on in some other place in the world to try and save the little victims of this horrible, unjust, unforgiving, unrelenting disease.

Research in Britain, America, Germany, Canada and Australia was the hope for tomorrow. But it was already too late to save Charly and perhaps Rhys.

Scientists were working full-time to uncover the cause of Batten's disease, to delineate the biochemical mechanisms underlying its pathology, to devise accurate methods of detection and diagnosis, to seek clues to effective treatment and, above all, develop tools for prevention through genetic counselling.

It was all about chromosome 1 or 12 or 16 or something, genes and DNA and ... Barry's mind clouded over and he fell asleep at last.

Barry had always refused to take no for an answer, even from top specialists who said his son could never be saved. He had volunteered Rhys for the first-ever bone marrow transplant on a Batten's disease victim and he knew it was a risk. He and Carmen had been put in touch with Professor John Hobbs at London's Westminster Children's Hospital, home of Europe's leading, specialised, bone marrow transplant unit. It was here that Professor Hobbs had pioneered the first transplants in the battle against some of the world's rare metabolic diseases. He was the one man in Barry and Carmen's world who was willing to take a chance with a transplant on Rhys. His decision had been based on long and accurate research and there was hope at last for the couple who were beginning to despair.

A search of the world's bone marrow register to find a suitable, unrelated donor for Rhys got under way. A month later, three compatible donors were found. Then came the long, agonising wait. A medical ethics review committee had to give its approval because of the experimental nature of the operation. Such committees move slowly. For five months Barry and Carmen spent one sleepless night after another, hoping their son would be given the chance of survival.

Then, in November 1992, a team of doctors at the Westminster, headed by Dr Ashok Vellodi, received the permission everyone had been waiting for. It should have been a celebration. But with the good news came the bad. In a telephone call Barry and Carmen learned that Health Secretary Virginia Bottomley had closed the hospital – to cut government spending. It would be replaced by a new, showpiece medical centre – but it would not have a transplant unit, because the building costs were already over budget. Barry and Carmen were devastated.

The couple didn't even get a letter to warn them. No alternative was offered. Rhys was the only child promised a transplant at the hospital only to be turned away with no hope. It wasn't just Batten's disease that was Barry and Carmen's enemy, it was the Tory Government as well. How could it put a price on their son's life, how heartless could it be?

Barry felt the door to life had been slammed in his son's face by callous, Whitehall bureaucrats and so he took Health Secretary Virginia Bottomley to court – and won. He left no stone unturned. He tracked down experts on the disease in America, Italy, Russia, Korea and South Africa.

The scientists and doctors were trying to isolate the exact genetic defect in the four types of Batten's disease. They were also trying to prevent the propagation of the illness by identifying carriers and those most at risk. By genetic testing they planned to treat potential patients like Rhys early, before signs and symptoms developed. Gene replacement therapy or enzyme replacement treatment held the answer. It was all within the realms of scientific knowledge and expertise. But it was the funding that held up the desperate hope of a cure.

Money was coming in, however, and the trickle of cash was becoming a steady stream as the world grew more aware of the condition.

Research centres at Indiana University, New York State University, the University of Chicago, Massachusetts General Hospital and London's Rayne's Institute were in the forefront of the race to save Batten's disease victims.

At Indiana University the most recent advances in research indicated that the infantile strain of the disease was caused by a genetic defect on chromosome 1 and the juvenile form was caused by a defect on chromosome 16. They were already isolating the genes, a labour-intensive and expensive task. The process was being helped by families supplying blood and tissues as sources of DNA for study. The university had set up a tissue bank with 100 cell lines available to anyone investigating the disease in the world.

The whole idea was given a boost when the Biosafety Committee of America's National Institute of Health approved a proposal to treat children with a severe genetic disease by inserting new genes into their blood cells. Everyone's ultimate goal was to prevent the ravages of this terrible illness. The same gene therapy was being used to treat, and it was hoped cure, children with another life-threatening genetic illness, cystic fibrosis.

But the bottom line was that Batten's disease, first described as long ago as 1826, remained devastating, unexpected, progressive, incurable, costly to treat, difficult to diagnose, of unknown cause, unpreventable, degenerative and fatal at an early age.

For Barry and Carmen and other parents like them, the battles to save their children were impossible to win. But the war against the disease was only just beginning. So far Barry had won every skirmish in the battle to get things done. Every time, so far, except this last and most painful fight.

Rhys's first bone marrow transplant had failed because his own original marrow had fought and won over the healthy implant. Now a needle had been found in a haystack. A new donor had been discovered. Friday had to work. It just had to. And that day he would be with Carmen. He would tell her he was sorry about the rows, about the tension. He would make it up, somehow.

Rhys opened his eyes to a hug from his mother.

He had suffered diarrhoea all through the night and all through the morning. Carmen hadn't slept at all.

Finally Rhys drifted off to sleep again and Carmen did too. It was eleven o'clock in the morning and she slept until one that afternoon.

Carmen didn't have an appetite when she woke up, but Rhys was ravenous and gobbled down two hospital sausages, served up by the wonderful ladies from the hospital's catering staff who worked so closely with the dietitians. The children in their care like Rhys could not eat anything fresh such as vegetables and fruit because of the bacteria in them. Out of all the yoghurts on the market only one had been approved as being totally bacteria-free. It was a tricky job. Carmen was grateful to them for doing it. One day she would help others. One day somehow.

Carmen stared around the brightly painted flat with its blue nylon curtains, red carpet floors and functional furniture. It was her and Barry's home for a while. A place to be near their son while he underwent the vital bone marrow transplant that could save his life.

Tonight her little son would go into isolation to prepare him for the treatment. It was Friday, 19 August 1994. She had tried to explain to him what would happen, but he didn't properly understand. She got dressed and dressed Rhys and then they went into town. He parked his little bicycle outside the Disney store where they bought a *Winnie the Pooh* video and a *Pinocchio* book Rhys wouldn't put down. Carmen looked at her watch. She and Barry had wanted some time together with their son and it was time to get back to the flat.

Barry swept Rhys up in his arms as they walked through the front door.

'All right, I'll read *Pinocchio* to you, but it's bathtime first,' he said carrying him off.

Carmen brought Barry in a mug of tea as he soaked in the bath with his son. Then they dressed him in his blue pyjamas and Batman socks ready for the isolation unit.

At 6.30 p.m., the nurse, Trina, arrived in the sealed unit with an array of drugs – Pethidine, hydrocortisone and Ondansetron. The names didn't mean anything to Carmen. She just held her breath as Trina fed them into Rhys's 'wiggly' one after the other, trusting his mum and dad. 'Wiggly' was the hospital's nickname for the Hickman line. There was even a comic book featuring the line as a cartoon character named Wiggly, just to get the children used to it, to accept it as a friend.

An hour later, as they sat looking at Rhys in his bed, the marrow arrived. It had been donated by a woman who wanted to remain anonymous. Rhys had written her a thank-you card and she was visibly moved when a nurse had given it to her earlier that day. She had known who the marrow was for, but she was too shy to be introduced to Barry and Carmen.

The doctors had spent the last ten days preparing Rhys's immune system to accept the implant of new bone marrow. Now this was it. Carmen stood in her surgical mask watching the marrow drip into Rhys's Hickman line in the isolation cubicle, minute after minute, hour after hour.

Rhys's little blue socks were in her handbag. She couldn't bear to look at them because seeing them was painful. She didn't know why she had brought them along, but just knowing she had them was a comfort.

The nurse interrupted Carmen's thoughts. It was midnight and a present had just been delivered from the TV station GMTV – a giant panda with a note saying: 'Good luck Rhys . . . and good luck Barry, Carmen and Charly!'

Barry and Carmen returned to the flat to snatch a few hours' rest. During the night the orange liquid dripping into Rhys's body would be checked every fifteen minutes by Dawn who was Rhys's named nurse, and who had been such a strength to Barry and Carmen during their son's first transplant in July 1993.

The next morning, Carmen woke and drew the curtains wondering if she had overslept. Everything must have been all right or the nurses would have got her up.

She looked out at the dismal day, the rain painting the old Victorian buildings across the road a sombre grey. She showered and changed into a pair of Levi jeans and at 6.45 a.m. she was at her son's side again, staring down through the transparent isolation covers as he slept peacefully on. The telephone rang and woke Rhys up. By the time Carmen had got out his favourite toy of the moment, Waffle Castle, he was hungry. She fed him porridge and he complained of a stomach ache.

'It's the drugs,' said Dawn.

Suddenly Rhys was tired again. They put away the building bricks and he fell asleep almost immediately. When he woke up again he was hungry. More sausages and bread and hot chocolate were dished up and rapidly disappeared off his plate.

All in all it was a bad afternoon. Rhys grew poorly, sleeping in fits and starts, holding his stomach, complaining of cramps and there was more diarrhoea.

'Don't worry, he's a strong little boy, a plucky little thing,' said Dawn.

Carmen stroked her son's head. Poor little soul, she thought. Still, he was healthy, so far. Her thoughts wandered to Charly. She was staying with Barry's cousin Julie, so she was OK. They got on fine. Carmen loved her kids to death. But even with all the tragedy and heartbreak and worry, all she could say to herself was that it was a funny old world. 'Yes, it's a funny old world,' she finally said out loud and wrote the words in her diary.

That evening in the flat Barry and Carmen sat together on the sofa until late. They talked about Rhys and Charly and all the things they loved about them. How much fun they were . . . or Charly had been. How loving they were and how gentle. As they huddled together in front of the glow from the bars of a little electric fire, Carmen felt like she and Barry were in a lifeboat, afraid, alone, clinging to each other in stormy waters, wondering if they would find land again and see their loved ones. She felt adrift. Their son was in an isolation ward and not upstairs tucked up in his bed with his Superman posters on the wall. Their daughter was hundreds of miles away in Essex and they could not quickly get to her side or kiss her goodnight, or tuck her up . . . and time was running out to do those things that other people just took for granted.

Carmen desperately wanted to go home. She wanted their house to come alive again. She wanted to hear the sound of banging doors, of boiling kettles, of children's laughter . . . of Barry playing his guitar or complaining he couldn't find his socks or shirts. They fell asleep together on the sofa as they had done so many times. Barry woke around 3 a.m. and put a blanket over Carmen, not wanting to wake her. He had to make sure Rhys was OK, so he walked back up to the hospital for a last check before going to bed.

On Sunday Carmen went to the isolation unit at 6.45 in the morning while Barry was still asleep in the flat. He had woken up but lay staring at the ceiling, too tired to get up. He planned to go in around 10 a.m. after collecting some cash from the bank.

It was a warm, muggy morning and it began to rain softly, the slightly sticky rain of early summer. He enjoyed the walk down to the high street. Bristol's tourists, now all year round, had put up their brollies and were drifting along the shiny, wet pavements in exasperating, aimless hordes, the pointed ends of their umbrellas at eye level. They infuriated him.

The rain was getting heavier. He reached the top of the hill, turned his collar up and ran across the green lawn at the back of the hospital grounds and made his way through a clump of trees which were the only living things around looking grateful for the rain. As he made his way into the hospital, a young couple went past him huddled together and giggling under an old newspaper they were attempting to use as an umbrella. Barry wondered if Rhys would ever have a girlfriend like that. He put the thought out of his mind.

When he arrived, Carmen left to go shopping.

Rhys was bright and breezy. He had slept well all night. The doctors were pleased. Barry spent the morning playing games with him. It was a good day. Barry was optimistic. Rhys slept a little and tucked into beans on toast for lunch and sausages and chips for dinner. Crisps and biscuits came in between. At around 8 p.m. he fell asleep while playing with his Action Man gun, shooting at imaginary cowboys and Indians around his bed, as Barry tried to read *Pinocchio* and *Fireman Sam* to him. Carmen went back to the flat to cook a meal, but she couldn't eat, even the thought of eating was too exhausting for her. She put a lasagne in the oven for Barry and returned to her son's side. That's how it was, a sort of rota system. They felt like they were on remote control, and they missed Charly terribly. They were desperate to get back to her side. She needed their love too.

Carmen watched as Dawn hooked Rhys up for a blood transfusion. She wondered how much more her son could take.

The news bulletins covering Rhys's condition ran throughout the day. Barry did a string of interviews for Sky TV, the BBC, ITN, HTV and GMTV. Everyone seemed really concerned.

'Have some of this, Bottomley!' he said to himself, as he returned to his son's side. He could not bring himself to forgive the Secretary of State for Health or the Government for the despair he felt they had caused him and Carmen and parents like them by closing the transplant unit at London's Westminster Children's Hospital.

He looked out of the hospital corridor window down at the hordes of reporters camped outside. Didn't it ever occur to them, he wondered, that he had to be with Rhys and see Rhys through? He couldn't keep coming out to do interviews and pose for pictures. He knew that they were all decent people trying to do their jobs, but *they* were working in shifts, replacing each other and bringing each other bacon butties. He felt like an animal in a zoo. The only thing that kept his temper even was that what he and Carmen were doing might help other families like them. He needed the media to keep up public awareness of the plight of victims of Batten's disease as much as they needed him for a news story.

Rhys had lost his appetite, but the doctors didn't seem too worried. They were more concerned about his diarrhoea that just wouldn't go away, although it was easing.

The next day things took a turn for the worse. Rhys woke about 7.15 a.m. and he was grumpy. His mouth was dry and sore. Barry managed to get him to swallow some hot chocolate, but he wouldn't eat and cried with the stomach pains. There was more diarrhoea too.

Dr Michael Barrett came to see him and prescribed some medicines for his sore mouth. Rhys was suffering from the expected side effects of the chemotherapy. The day then went in fits and starts. Sometimes Rhys slept, sometimes he snuggled into the armchair by his bed and looked around the room, sometimes the nurse played with his legs, rubbing them and lifting them up to keep them active, sometimes he grew grumpy again and cried.

Carmen shouted out and Barry dropped the music magazine he was reading. Rhys's blood line had come off as he slumped down in the chair falling asleep. Blood was pumping everywhere from his plastic tubes – it looked like gallons.

'Nurse!' Barry screamed, not knowing what to do as he held his son. The nurse arrived and quickly re-attached the tube into the Hickman line. Barry and Carmen's stomachs were going over. They had felt so helpless. The nurse reassured them. It was only the equivalent of a cupful of blood and the human body held eight pints. Barry felt sick with worry and Carmen broke down and cried.

Next came the orals: an assortment of pills and liquids that Rhys's body so desperately needed. But because of his sore mouth, every pill was agony. Carmen could hardly watch.

In the night it rained. Carmen lay awake in Barry's arms as he slept, listening to the raindrops falling on the leaves of the eucalyptus trees and evergreen bushes outside. She visualised the grateful grass and flowers and the shining wet stones of the terraces and pavements leading to the hospital doors. She lay very still, conscious of her husband sleeping, conscious of her quite unspeakable sadness. Her little boy wasn't far away . . . but far away enough. She had a feeling, a feeling that this was just the beginning of another new chapter in her life. She wanted to see her son have sons and their sons have sons. She wanted Barry and herself and Rhys and Charly to go on being a family. Her eyes closed and when she opened them again it was morning.

It was 6.30 a.m. Outside the sky held the promise of a warm summer's day, the sort that drew people out to riverside pubs and garden patios, where rusting barbecue trolleys filled the air with the smell of charcoal and burnt sausages. Barry stirred and opened his eyes, still sleepy. He looked at Carmen. She was lying on the bed, staring at the ceiling with tears in her eyes.

Her fists were clenched tight as if she was going to smash an imaginary enemy. He knew she was willing her son to live.

'His life is in the hands of the doctors now,' he said. 'Good doctors.'

Carmen didn't answer. She was remembering how it had all begun.

2: The Great Adventure

Barry felt the kiss on his brow. But he didn't know it was a kiss. He just felt something soft. Through the bandages across his head he could make out the blurred shapes around his bed as the first pink streaks of dawn seeped through the hospital curtains. He didn't know his father, who had virtually slept at his side for seven days since he had been in a coma, had just kissed him. He didn't know the nurse was there checking the tubes coming out of his arm and nose like tentacles. He could only hear the dull bleep of a heart monitor. He didn't know what it was and he didn't want to. He drifted in and out of his dreamlike visions without a care in the world.

His bicycle. The hill that wound down from his house. Faster, faster. Look no hands. Turning the corner now. Blackness. Barry murmured and his father leant over him. But it was nothing. His father slumped back in the chair, rubbing his eyes.

His eleven-year-old son had been in a coma for seven days. He was looking for a sign that it would all soon be over. At first Barry's mother was so upset she couldn't bring herself to visit.

Barry had left his school coat at his friend's house

just down the hill and around the corner from his home.

'Don't be long – tea's on,' his mother shouted, as he sped off on his bicycle to pick up the black school blazer.

Auntie Josie, who lived three doors away, waved and tutted as he sped down the hill with no hands on the handlebars of his Raleigh racer. Barry was king of the road. Nothing could ever hurt him.

Then the screams rang out from mothers standing in front gardens as he turned the corner and smashed head-on into a car coming the other way. For a few seconds every one was stunned. The images of Barry's crumpled bike beside his motionless body, the blood on the kerbstone, the face of the shocked driver were frozen in time.

Unconscious, bruised and battered, he was rushed to nearby St Margaret's Hospital. He had a broken shoulder and a fractured skull and lay in a coma but luckily he survived. After he broke through the fragile veil between him and the world, he opened his eyes and asked for his brother David. His father wondered why they were his first words. The two of them had never really seemed to get on, always fighting as young brothers do. His father needn't have worried though. They were to become close friends and allies in the turbulent years to come.

A few weeks later Barry was back at Epping Junior School, much to the amazement of his schoolfriends.

'We thought you was dead!' said one. 'The class said a prayer for you!'

'Nuh, I was just sleeping.'

From that day on Barry's nickname was Danny Dormouse. The only person who never laughed at the joke was Barry's mother Rosie.

Barry never forgot the near-fatal accident, but it did not stop him from taking chances in his life. He came to believe that he was born to live on the edge and it was that dare-devil streak in him that would one day give his children every fighting chance for survival.

Barry Patrick Daniels was born on 15 May 1958 at Thorpe Coombe Hospital, Walthamstow, East London. The same hospital was to be the birthplace nine years later of his future wife Carmen.

His father Bill worked in the Greater London Council's accounts department at County Hall. The family lived in Cuthbert Road, Walthamstow, a neat row of terraced houses running down to the railway line that curled into Liverpool Street Station in the heart of the City. They shared the house with his mother's brother Charlie and his wife Josie. His mother had four brothers and a sister. The whole clan, who lived locally, were a typical East London family.

When Barry was eighteen months old, the family moved to a third-floor flat nearby where they stayed for nearly three years before moving out to the country – and another world.

Barry began to notice the sunsets. He fished and played tag in Epping Forest with his new friends. He played football in the park and rode his bike over the mud paths in the countryside. As he grew older, evenings were spent at a local disco, rocking to a band.

Barry hated his school, living only for his music. He spent hours in his little back bedroom poring over guitar instruction books written by the legendary Bert Weedon and strumming 'Mama's Gonna Buy Me A Mocking Bird' on a battered old Spanish six-string. The noise drove his parents mad. His father wished him all the best with his music but was not interested enough to try and understand it.

At school Barry's enthusiasm was never really aroused for any subject, although he was good at art and music. He loved writing stories and was often complimented on his imagination, but his grammar was poor.

On one occasion fourth-year pupils wrote an essay to be read out in class. Barry wrote a sexy story with lots of rude bits in it. It was science fiction, about an alien ravishing young, innocent Earth girls. His English teacher kept his book and refused to let the story be read out, ignoring the pleas and cheers of support from Barry's classmates.

At this time, Barry's superhero was David Bowie. The rock star had a huge influence on Barry's music – and his appearance. Barry dyed his hair in an assortment of colours and had it cropped to the same Bowie style. His father thought this man Bowie would be the end of his son. Then things went further. Barry and his best friend Mick Jessop, another Bowie freak, became the first boys in the school to have their ears pierced – they were just thirteen.

The theatre was packed and there was an air of expectancy in the audience of screaming rock fans. The noise was deafening.

'Ladies and gentlemen, a cheer please for Freeway, the band that is setting Epping Forest alight.'

The audience erupted, the curtain rose and there was Barry, in tight white jeans and a black and silver lurex top, hanging over a microphone.

Inside he felt this was it. The nerves, the screaming, the cheers, the sounds of rock'n'roll. He felt he was living on the edge.

Barry's group came second in the Essex Battle of the Bands talent contest that night at the Victoria Theatre in Southend-on-Sea. The audience had been rocked by a twenty-minute session of original material, much of it written by Barry. It was a moment he would never forget. He was just fifteen.

Freeway had been formed at the Centrepoint Youth Club in Epping by Barry and his schoolmate Jeff Reeves, nicknamed JR. But it was a pretty young girl named Lavinia who gave the group its heart. Barry was infatuated with her. It had been love at first sight and from that moment on she seemed to influence his music. It was Lavinia who put them on the road to the Victoria Theatre that memorable night.

As it was obvious he was never going to be a brain surgeon or prime minister, Barry left school the following year and got a job as a messenger boy. But like most boys at that age, he was restless and couldn't settle down to his new life. He dreamed of being a rock star and couldn't wait to get to the disco or shut himself away in the bedroom of his home with his records and write songs with his old school pal Mick, a tall, gangly lad just like himself. He drifted from one job to the next, never feeling it was for him. All he wanted was enough money to pay for his records, his amplifiers and guitar strings.

The sun blistered Barry's back as he sat on a pile of new red bricks and he slipped on a T-shirt before flicking through a copy of the *Sun*. He stopped at page three, mostly because of the picture of the shapely, topless blonde lying on Brighton beach. The summer of 1976 was a scorcher – just like her.

He put his feet up on an upturned bucket at the back of the half-built house with its window frames held in by huge wooden wedges. Sod this for a game of soldiers, he thought. How much more could he stand working on a building site? He began to hum the words of a new song he had been working on and dream of his new Ovation guitar. The ebony wood, hand-made acoustic had cost him £700 on HP, but it was worth every penny, even if his dear old mum did end up helping him with the debt. The image of it faded in his mind as he dozed off in the sunshine.

'Oi! What's your game?'

Barry opened his eyes, trying to focus in the sunshine.

'I told you before – you're just bloody lazy. You're fired!' The site foreman kicked away the bucket from under his feet.

A week later, jobless Barry went with the family clan for its usual holiday bash. This time it was the Atherfield Bay holiday camp on the Isle of Wight. Sun, sea, sex and Scotch was the recipe for paradise. The rock'n'roll nights were squeezed between bouts of bingo and booze. Barry was having so much fun he didn't want to leave and neither did his cousin Peter. The young builder from Stevenage was out of work too.

On a sweltering hot Saturday morning they stood in the car park waving goodbye to the clan as one by one they boarded the coach for the ferry home. Barry and Peter had managed to get themselves jobs in the camp kitchen. From here on it was the young man's dream.

Barry turned to Peter.

'Let's have a pint and toast our luck . . . from now on it's sunshine, booze and women all the way!'

The dream continued for two long summers and it was during that time that Barry was to meet a man who would become a lifelong friend. Lin, an American from the state of South Dakota, was working as a maintenance and odd-job man at the camp. They would spend many a long, hot summer afternoon in the staff quarters surrounded by cans of cold beer playing their guitars and singing rock songs until they were drunk and the words just didn't make sense any more. One day Lin would open a door to a new chapter in Barry's life.

Late in August 1977 Barry returned to Epping and met another person who was to change his path in life. Chris Sutton was sixteen and had just arrived in England from New Zealand. The tall, long-haired keyboard player was a gifted singer and songwriter too. He and Barry clicked at their first meeting in the local pub. Within weeks they had formed a five-piece band called Gemini.

The lads were excited. They sounded good, influenced by the sounds of Elton John and, of course, David Bowie. And their numbers were original, written by Barry or Chris or both.

In April 1978, they drove through the rain to the Rockstar studios in London, run by ex-Gary Glitter band member Jon Springate, to record a demo of their work. The playback rocked them. They thought they were sensational. Stardom was on the way. But the stardom dream was to fade like stardust. Months of pounding the pavements searching for that elusive recording contract were repaid by worn-out heels and aching tendons. Barry and the boys just didn't have the experience it took to open doors. They needed guidance but couldn't get any. They were just a bunch of hopeful teenagers with a rock'n'roll dream. They thought stardom would come to them out of the blue. Instead, they were left just feeling blue. Still, at least they hadn't made the mistake that Barry's pal Tim, who taught him to play the guitar, had made. Tim had been playing with a bunch of musicians but didn't bother to pursue it and decided to teach guitar at music college instead. The lads he had been playing with went on to call themselves Dire Straits, one of the biggest rock bands to hit the charts in the 1980s.

Late in August that year, Chris signed an independent publishing deal. Barry's dream was over. There were no hard feelings. That was life. Chris was his great friend. He wished him all the luck in the world. They managed to find time together to play as a duet called Blue Beach in the George and Dragon pub in Epping to earn extra cash – and even did some working men's clubs together. But things were never to be the same again. Barry signed an independent publishing deal with Jet Records, but that turned sour after the first year.

At first, however, Barry was optimistic. Maybe Jet was the turning point. It was then that he ran into Lavinia, his boyhood fantasy again. It all seemed so perfect. His heart strings were playing louder than his guitar strings and he moved in with her. She was separated from her husband and had two lovely children, Jane and Richard, whom Barry idolised. Life was good for a while, but by the end of the year he had become despondent. His songs lost their direction and the publishers weren't pleased. He and Lavinia argued time and again. Finally, the relationship crashed along with the deal with Jet. Barry knew he needed a change in his life, a big, big change.

Bill stood in the lounge sipping a mug of tea.

'You know, son, your mother and I don't want you to go.'

'I know, dad,' said Barry, putting his hand on his father's shoulder. 'But I'm so pissed off with the English way of life, I just have to get out.'

It was March 1980. Bill looked at the Ovation guitar in its case and the old kitbag in the hallway. He knew his son wanted a change in his way of life. A big change. But Bill had to think of Rosie. Mothers and sons and all that. There was a special bonding. He understood why his son had to go. He would too if he was younger and had the chance. But Barry's mother . . . well . . .

It was the hardest thing, saying goodbye to his mother, but Barry knew she understood deep inside. Funny, he hadn't even told his brother David. But then, they never did see very much of each other anyway.

The next morning Barry was walking across the tarmac to board a plane for America. He turned and waved to Chris staring down from the terminal building window. Barry would miss him a lot. They had such a great friendship. He would miss his mother and father too — they were really close. He would never meet better people in the world. But now the great adventure had begun. There were no second thoughts. No looking back.

It was a bright, sunny March morning when the Greyhound bus, covered in dust from the South Dakota desert, dropped Barry in Sioux Falls. The city, founded in 1857 and named after the tumbling falls of the Big Sioux River, was the largest in the state. The huge granite rocks and trees along the river banks were once used to construct the old city buildings before the railroad arrived and, with it, freight-loads of cement. The city was now a sprawling glass and concrete metropolis that would have made the legendary Indian warrior and leader of the Sioux, Chief Sitting Bull, turn in his grave. The Sioux Indians once roamed the plains the Greyhound buses now sped over, hunting buffalo in freedom before the white man came.

Barry rang Lin from the dusty, yellow telephone box. His friend from the Atherfield Bay holiday camp was now married to a South Dakota girl named Annie. They lived on a pig farm in a small town of just 200 people called Mission Hill, five miles outside Yankton. Within an hour Lin was making the 110-mile journey to Sioux Falls in his battered old Chevrolet pick-up truck to collect Barry. During the trip back they reflected on the great times they had with his cousin Peter in 1977, as they sped across the red rock plains to Mission Hill, watching the March light shimmer from gold to silver to grey.

Barry was overwhelmed with the hospitality he received from the people of the small American town of timber and concrete houses. Lin's one-bedroom home, however, was too small for him to stay in so he slept in a 30 ft camper parked next to the pig sties. Barry didn't mind; he was going with the flow and having such a good time that he quickly adjusted to the smells around him and the grunting of the pigs through the night. Annie served up fried steak and chips by the shovel load. They all ate with gusto every night, laughing, talking and drinking on the porch in the moonlight. Life was good.

For the next few weeks Barry went to farm auctions, where wearing a baseball cap was almost compulsory, helped pull the teeth of the baby piglets and generally mucked in. The area was one of the largest livestock markets in the United States. Being covered in pig swill was a million miles away from why he had come to America. But for a while his musical dream could wait.

This was President Jimmy Carter's America. Barry sipped cold beers in the bars and watched life go by. The men who leant against their trucks, drinking cans of Budweiser in the sunshine, talking, passing around the odd joint, all seemed hard, masculine, muscular, tough, sexy young men, full of health and laughter. They were all young studs. They weren't studying to be doctors or reading English Literature or training to be chartered accountants or saving with a building society for the deposit on a house. This wasn't at all like England. The dismal, grey England he wanted to get away from. They didn't moan about income tax or unemployment, or worry about having the latest designer suit. They were honest-to-goodness working-class men who loved their Budweisers, their motorbikes, their Levi jeans and T-shirts, their trucks, their farms and their women. They had no ambition to go to Europe, dine at the Ritz or take pictures of Number 10 Downing Street. They didn't read books, see plays or discuss last night's TV documentary. These were people living in a basic world. Barry felt at home.

He fished in the James River, ploughed the land driving a tractor for the first time in his life and breathed in the fresh, crisp air. He felt closer to nature than he had ever done. When he had left London for Epping as a boy he thought he was in the country — but this was real country. This was the rural life at its best.

He liked the Indians too. When he first arrived he had been warned never to run out of petrol or break down while driving through one of their reservations. But he found he enjoyed their company and sympathised with their problems. They felt cheated by the white Americans of what was rightfully theirs like the beautiful Black Hills where buffalo still roamed free.

And now Barry roamed free too – on Lin's bicycle. Nearly every day he would pedal five miles along dusty dirt roads to the bustling town of Yankton where he made new friends, like office-worker John Murray, from the Chamber of Commerce, a cool, confident American with a dry sense of humour and an insatiable appetite for bourbon and burgers.

But nothing lasts for ever and before long Barry had to make a decision. After a couple of months his money ran out and it looked certain he would have to return to England. Then his luck changed, thanks to John. As they sat one morning pouring ketchup over their burgers in the diner, Barry told his friend that the money well was running dry.

'I really came to the States for my music,' said Barry, 'but I've made no progress with my songs and I need to earn money. I can't stay with Lin for ever. I guess I'll have to book my ticket back to London next week.'

John went to the telephone and returned with a huge smile on his face.

'What's so funny?' Barry asked.

'You're going to be a radio star,' his friend replied.

John knew a producer on the local radio station KYNT and had fixed up a live interview over the air for Barry the next day. They wanted to play his songs and talk to him about his music. Barry felt the nerves and excitement gnaw at the burger in his stomach.

The interview went well the next day. Barry told how his best friend was his Ovation guitar and of the years he had spent writing songs, many of them now influenced by his life in Dakota. His demo discs were played between the chats and when he walked out of the dimly lit studio into the bright sunlight he felt ten feet tall. At least America had heard his music.

It was a good story – an Englishman who had turned up in America with a musical dream. Within days Barry had offers to join rock bands. The one he chose was a group called Winterset, whose drummer Rick Schramm was also a DJ at KYNT. The dream was coming true and Barry would never forget the buzz he felt when he arrived to play his first gig – at Yankton, the town that had made him so welcome.

It was a dry, sticky afternoon on 23 May 1980, when Barry walked into the club Kochi for the final soundcheck, burger in one hand and guitar in the other. He stopped for a moment and read the poster on the wall. It said: 'Presenting Winterset featuring Barry Daniels'. He smiled to himself – his musical dream was coming true at last.

The show had been widely advertised in newspapers and on the radio and a special set had been created for the guest appearance of the guitar-strumming Englishman. The band rehearsed Barry's act for days. It was based around his original numbers, written while he had been preparing for his trip to the States over the last six months, dreaming of his American adventure.

It was the big night and there was a full house. Barry felt he had a lot to thank Yankton for. Minutes before he walked on stage he felt the nerves tearing his stomach apart. He remembered the talent contest at the old Victoria Theatre in Southend. A line from his favourite David Bowie song, 'Time', kept repeating itself in his mind: 'Time, he's waiting in the wings . . . he thinks of senseless things . . . his script is you and me boy!' Bowie must have experienced these same nerves in his early days, Barry thought to himself.

Rick crashed a cymbal and did a roll on the drums and it snapped him out of his thoughts.

'Ladies and gentlemen . . . if there are any . . . may I present the band Winterset and Barry Daniels, a great rock'n'roll star direct from London, England,' said the presenter in his red leather cowboy boots and stetson hat. Rick winked at Barry, but Barry, wearing an American Army shirt with 'I Love America' and the wings of an eagle across the front and a huge figure one on the back embroidered with a Union Jack, didn't even have time to smile. Within seconds he was strapping on his guitar and saying hello to the audience through the applause.

He banged the strings hard, switching from C to F major and back again. The Barry Daniels show had begun. Another great adventure.

Later, in the early hours of the morning, Barry lay awake on his bed in Rick's house, the memories and sounds of the night buzzing through his mind. They liked him, they really did. They liked his songs. One day he would write a song that would capture the hearts of everyone. He swore it to himself. Little did he know then that such a song would be sparked by tragedy.

In the months that followed Barry settled in at Yankton, living with Rick and his wife Linda. A great friendship was being bonded and although he didn't know it, they would always be there for him in the tragic years ahead. He played gig after gig with the boys in Winterset – Rick, Pos, Chuck, Bob, Dorean and Tommy – and even got a job coaching the local Mount Marty college soccer team. Breakfast was often in a tea-shop on Main Street run by Liz Sheils and her daughter Christine. Liz was an Englishwoman who had brought a quaint Devonshire atmosphere to the dry, arid, Middle West of America.

Barry had many friends in Yankton, but he never got caught up in any long-term, romantic relationships. Being a rock'n'roll star had its rewards, however, and there was never any shortage of sexy American girls. Being English also had its advantages. They found his accent quaint.

Then, one shapely brunette, who always seemed to be at his shows, asked him to have afternoon tea with her at Liz's place.

Kim was the all-American girl. The California girl. The girl that would turn the heads of every man on the beach. Barry was flattered.

'The show was great last night,' she said, sipping her coffee and staring across the table at him.

'I'm pleased you were there. It's nice to hear what people have to say about the act,' he replied, wondering why she had invited him out. Not that he minded. Quite the opposite. Anyway, he was going with the flow.

'You must know I'm not just interested in your music.'

Barry tried to stay cool, look cool, even though he had that feeling. The feeling of a young man hunting for adventure. 'Oh, really.'

'Yes, really. I'd like to see more of you – without your . . . without your guitar.'

Barry nearly fell off his chair.

'Oh, right,' he said.

'Would you like to come away with me for a long weekend?'

Barry couldn't believe what he was hearing. Were all American girls so forward? He had never been

propositioned like that before. How could he say no?
'Love to!'
'OK then, Las Vegas, here we come.'

It was a non-stop weekend in more ways than one. Barry loved the glittering, gambling city nestling in the desert of southeastern Nevada. Once again, it was an experience that made him feel restless. For four days he never slept: Kim, the gambling machines, the night life, the glitz, the stars, the prostitutes, the villains, the Mafia, the shows, the Martinis by the pitcherful he threw down the sink because they had stood so long they had become diluted with ice, the endless eating of peanut-butter cookies. He stood and shouted his adoration for Frank Sinatra in Caesar's Palace. He swam in pools as the desert heat hit 120 degrees. He played blackjack at the Sands Hotel and he laughed and felt freer than he had ever done before. He adored the former railroad town that had grown from legalised gambling. He marvelled at the huge Hoover Dam to the east and the vast waters of Lake Mead. And he would remember for ever The Strip, the array of luxury hotels with their neon signs and casinos.

One evening back in Yankton, as he sat in a downtown bar drinking his fifth or sixth or seventh beer while the snow fell outside on the streets, he realised he had discovered something in Las Vegas he had been craving for – action. Midwest America, Yankton and Mission Hills was not giving him that edge. The edge he so badly needed. He needed more life, more glitz, more of everything. He felt the urge to travel west.

His last gig in Yankton was on Hallowe'en Night and the club was buzzing. He played his heart out as a farewell thank you to Winterset and the town for showing him the way. He owed his thanks to everybody and Lin and Annie more than most. For they had been there from the beginning.

Over breakfast the next morning Barry had a terrific headache and couldn't eat. He had consumed a whole bottle of bourbon the night before as well as the beers and then tried to get some sleep as the room spun slowly around him. Now just the thought of the yellow liquid made him feel nauseous. He was in no shape whatsoever to handle a three-day trip of several thousand miles. But he had to. He had to go to LA.

Barry stood for a few minutes at the Greyhound bus stop looking for the last time at the snow-covered streets of Yankton, a wonderful town and a wonderful community that had taken him under its wing and sheltered him from the storms of life. Now they had pointed the star-to-be in the inevitable direction of Los Angeles. Another big adventure was beginning.

Barry sat on the bus, still feeling like death, his knees against his chest and his feet on his bag as he headed 3,000 miles west to LA. He was humming to himself as he struggled to write a new song on the back of an old *National Enquirer* magazine. But the words wouldn't come right. His tongue was like sandpaper and his brain was a ball of cotton wool. He looked up at his guitar on the luggage rack, then out of the window. He didn't know why, but he felt uneasy. It was nothing to do with the hangover. Perhaps it was because he had no true stopping place in LA. He didn't know anyone there. He had nothing booked. He would be on the street, guitar case in one hand and an old bag of clothes in the other. He willed himself to ignore the monster within him that made him feel so scared. He was on the bus, in America, going with the flow through his own choice, he reasoned. Then someone sitting across the aisle from him said something that made the monster open its jaws and chew on him again.

'So you're going to LA and you're English,' said the fat American unwrapping another Havana cigar.

'Yes,' said Barry, not really wanting to talk.

'Music, huh! You play the guitar?'

'Yes, I've got a band. We've done really well so far.'

'Lots of killings up there,' said the American. 'It can get very ugly.'

But Barry really didn't want to talk and soon the man got the message.

The Greyhound bus was a weird way to travel. There were so many different kinds of people and so many changing faces on the trip. The first stop was Omaha, Nebraska, the heart of the Midwest. Then came Cheyenne, Wyoming, real cowboy country. It was an experience watching the faces of the people going about their business, never dreaming of leaving the town they were born in. And there was Barry, setting out, without a thought in the world of where he might end up, on yet another leg of his US adventure.

Three days later the morning sun lit up Los Angeles on the horizon and as the bus headed for the downtown Greyhound depot another elderly American man sitting opposite Barry leant over.

'So where you heading for, buddy?'

'I'm not sure yet. I haven't got any base.'

'Well, don't hang around the depot too long. There were 200 murders there last year – and the last one was only yesterday.'

Barry was lost for words. He wasn't sure if the American was winding him up or whether he was for real. But he wasn't taking any chances. It was the second time he had been told about the killings. He got off the Greyhound and immediately boarded a local bus to Santa Anna and the beach area. Nothing could stop him now. Before the 35-minute journey was over he had chatted up a young American girl who offered him a place to stay. Barry didn't care where or with whom. He just needed a base.

Once again everything worked out well and the offer gave him a week to find his way around – although the apartment was on the edge of Lafayette Park, an area notorious for muggings, rape and murder. Barry liked living on the edge – but not that edge. And the girl seemed strange. She was quiet, withdrawn and wouldn't allow him a key. He would often spend hours on the landing waiting for her to return and open the door. He wondered if she was a female serial killer. Something about her chilled him to the bone and he was determined to break free of her web.

Just like Las Vegas, he adored LA, a sprawling city that curled its way along the coastal plain between the San Gabriel Mountains and the Pacific Ocean.

Barry had a special address on his list – the Motown building on Sunset and Vine. One afternoon, as bold as brass, he walked into Christian De-Walden's office at Zebra Music clutching his demo tape recorded in Yankton. Zebra liked it, in fact Barry thought it knocked them out. But that was Hollywood, although he didn't know it. Two hours later, he walked out through the glass doors feeling that the world was his oyster after signing a recording contract with studio time booked in Tinseltown. He turned to face the Santa Monica Mountains that towered over the city and stared at the famous Hollywood sign. Yes, he had finally arrived. Everything was working out. Nothing could stop him now. Sadly, he didn't know it, but he was on the Boulevard of Broken Dreams.

Barry gazed across the road at the young girl agitatedly trying to start her car. She obviously needed help and after a second look Barry thought she was definitely worth the effort. Nothing now for him was impossible. He walked over to her and tried to wave his magic wand.

'Hi. What's up? Can I help?'

She smiled, a sort of grateful smile. 'Yeah, if you can.'

He knew very little about cars, but this was his day. Within minutes he got it going. Ten minutes later they arrived at a coffee shop and talked and talked. Her name was Christina and she had just been to an audition as a singer at a club on Sunset Boulevard. She had travelled down from San Francisco just for the gig. As she was staying overnight Barry arranged to meet her at the Whisky A-Go-Go later that evening where The Stranglers were playing.

It turned out to be a great night. What more could he want? A gorgeous woman, a great band, lots of booze and a recording contract, all in one day. Their last stop was a nightcap at the Troubador Club on Doheny Drive, Beverly Hills. It was there that a struggling musician named Glenn Frey once sat and discussed the line-up for his new band, The Eagles, later to become one of the most famous groups in the world. Then it was back to Christina's hotel. What a wonderful city. What a wonderful night.

There was something about the early hours of the morning in Los Angeles as the sun broke over the Santa Monica Mountains. Barry walked slowly back to his apartment after breakfast. His dream was coming true. The dole queue in Epping was no alternative.

A week later he headed for the Will Rogers Park in Pacific Palisades.

The late Will Rogers was probably America's most famous cowboy, whose lasso techniques were legendary. His house was now a museum and his ranch a public park. Prince Charles had played polo there and the location was used many times as backdrops for movies. Barry had been told a lot of Britons gathered in the huge grounds to play football and generally make new friends. Soon Barry had made friends too – with Phil and Sean. Phil was from Ilford, in Essex, and was visiting a cousin who lived in Hollywood Hills. Sean was a native Californian of Irish stock; he played the guitar and worked for Bell Telecommunications. He appealed to Barry because he too dreamed of superstardom. The frustrated rock guitarist was always looking for that elusive break. Perhaps Sean held the key.

Barry moved in with Sean at his apartment on Ohio Avenue in West Hollywood. The days were spent writing music, rehearsing or lying on the beach with the Pacific Ocean roaring its way to the shore in the background. Then they would pop into the nearby King's Head pub for a pint. In the evening they would go clubbing with Lisa and Debbie, two girls who lived in the same apartment block. They did the whole circuit, Madam Wong's, Whisky A-Go-Go, the Troubador and the Roxy. Life now for Barry was far removed from the tranquillity of the Midwest and the nightlife of Yankton and its neighbouring towns. He woke up each morning to gleaming sunshine bursting through the leaves of the swaying palm trees. What a wonderful life, what a wonderful place. Heaven here on earth.

Within a month Barry and Sean had formed a

seven-piece band called The Stilletoes.

It seemed to Barry that the streets really were paved with gold as he pounded the pavement on Hollywood Boulevard in the footsteps of stars like Greta Garbo, Lon Chaney, Katherine Hepburn and Spencer Tracy. His mind flashed up images of wearing out his shoes in London, desperately searching for months for someone to open a door for him.

On a hot, sticky Friday morning Barry and Sean and the other lads in the band turned up at the Startrack studio in Hollywood, north-west of downtown Los Angeles, bounded by the foothills of the Santa Monica Mountains and Beverly Hills. Everything was going right. Production executives from Earth Wind and Fire were on hand to help – along with writer/producer Barry Hart from The Monkees. How could the project they were recording for the Japanese Music Festival go wrong? But, like everything else in Tinseltown, it was just a dream that never came true.

Barry sat by himself at the bar of the King's Head pub. He knew all the staff as he was a regular now. They were mostly from Britain. He was thinking about his recording contract that hadn't really come to anything yet when the noise from a crowd across the room broke his thoughts. He knew most of them, but not the olive-skinned brunette. God, she was beautiful, he thought. He couldn't help looking, trying to catch her glance. Finally he did, and she held his gaze, just for a few moments. Half an hour later she came to the bar to order a drink.

'Hi, my name's Barry.'

'Oh, you're English – you look so American.'

They laughed. Her name was Ginny and she asked

him where he was living. He gave her Sean's address and invited her to a barbecue the next day.

The next morning Barry played football in the park with Sean and Phil. Yes, he had invited a very special girl to the barbecue that evening. Yes, she was pretty. No, he couldn't tell them any more.

The night got off to a swing. The Stilletoes were working on a new set and they were all buzzin'. They could talk about nothing else. The Budweisers were flowing, the steaks sizzling on the grill, and the warm evening air was alive with the smell of charcoal.

When Ginny walked in, she captured the moment. She was centre stage. Every man at the party looked at her in her white, figure-hugging dress, at her olive complexion and her dark eyes. Barry was smitten. From that night on they saw each other every day.

Two weeks later on a beach in the moonlight as the Pacific breakers slapped against the shore, he proposed. It seemed so right for him. He needed a strong partner who could be there for him, to see him through his haphazard musical career. He needed some stability now.

Ginny's father was of Italian descent and the family home was in Bel Air, the swish part of LA. Barry found it difficult to adjust to their well-heeled lifestyle. It was a long way from Epping and his father's little greenhouse. They lived in a million-dollar mansion, with a swimming pool in the garden, in one of the most fashionable parts of Los Angeles, tucked away off Mulholland Drive in the hills overlooking the sprawling city. Ginny was beautiful and it was all about young love. The wedding drew closer.

Barry was worried that he would not be accepted by Ginny's parents. He was an English musician with an ear-ring in his right ear and blonde-streaked hair. But amazingly he got on well with his future in-laws. Ginny told him later that they liked him because he wasn't trying to prove anything. He was what he was. No false images. But could he live up to their expectations?

Barry pulled on the white trousers. It was a beautiful, hot sunny afternoon. Of all his dreams about rock'n'roll stardom, he had never imagined that he would one day have a society wedding. He was just a laid-back musician who only cared about the tension on his guitar strings and the problems he was having with the bridge section on his latest song. Now he was being swept away by some distant chords of a real-life love song. It was the biggest day of his life and he was just going with the flow. He had to go through with it now. No looking back. His mother and father had flown in with his cousin Mark just to be at the wedding. They were overwhelmed. If only they had known, and Ginny's parents had known, that the night before it was almost called off at the last minute because he and Ginny had a huge row. He had finally realised that they were two totally opposite people. But he had realised it too late. They both had strong, possessive natures which, together with a lack of communication and understanding provided the perfect ingredients for a fragile and potentially explosive relationship. It was to be a marriage destined for failure.

The ceremony on 30 May 1981 was a lavish affair. There were huge white and yellow floral displays at the small, beautiful chapel in nearby Westwood. Then came flowers and fountains and iced champagne at the garden party in Bel Air and an evening at the Beverly Hills Hilton, where special guest Christian De-Walden boasted about Barry's work for the Japanese

Music Festival to friends of Ginny's parents. Barry wasn't complaining. His parents were so proud of the little boy who had spent his life strumming a guitar in the bedroom, but they were wary of what problems both he and Ginny would face coming from such very different backgrounds.

In the wee small hours of the morning, Barry and Ginny jetted off to Las Vegas, the city of good memories for Barry. The future looked promising. Ginny had always had a lavish lifestyle and one day Barry would be able to provide that.

He tried hard. For the next few years he was on the LA road – recording, gigging, watching the dawn break through the windows of all-night coffee shops and bars. He slipped into the American way of life just like a native. There were ups and downs and, in the end, mostly downs. He loved Hollywood one day, and hated it the next. The American dream wasn't all it was cracked up to be. Too many music company executives trying to sign anybody and everybody just in case they had a new David Bowie. Barry got fed up trying. The rows with Ginny grew. The disillusion grew. In the end, he felt it was unfair to both of them to go on living as they were, with so much uncertainty.

The second of December 1984 was a miserable morning. In pouring rain, the cab picked Barry up from Ginny's parents' house and she stood watching from the front door. Barry felt confused, broken-hearted and mentally shattered. He couldn't even call home and explain what was happening. He didn't really know himself. He waved goodbye to Ginny through the rain-streaked window of the yellow cab as it pulled on to Mulholland Drive and sped away. Goodbye to Ginny and the life he knew in LA for the last time. It had all been a shattered dream. They had lived together for nearly four years. They were finally to get divorced in 1986.

Perhaps now Barry would find the edge he so desperately sought back home. But only more heartbreak was waiting. For the days with his father, whom he missed so much, were to be few.

3: All You Need Is Love

last time is Carmen stood waving goodbye in the hallway.
lived together before they finally moved
to parenthood in 19 .

Perhaps now Brian would find the edge he so
desperately sought back home. But only more
heartbreak was waiting. For the days with her father,
whom he adored so much, were to be few.

Carmen Mickleboro was born on 12 October 1967 at Thorpe Coombe Hospital, Walthamstow, East London. For her parents Sandra and camera-technician Brian she was the icing on the cake to a fairytale marriage. The bouncing baby with the cheeky little chuckle was the apple of their eye and went home to a house that had been turned into toyland. There were teddy bears and dolls in her bedroom, a rocking-horse in the hall and playmats and colouring books in the lounge. But within three years the fairytale had come to a sad end.

The bubbly toddler would pull the bedclothes over her head and cry at night, missing her father terribly. He had gone to work in Wellingborough, Northamptonshire, but her mother had refused to move home and now the couple, who had been together since they were fourteen, were drifting apart. On the rare occasions Brian came home, there weren't any arguments, just long silences. He was the kind of man who would rather ignore people than row. Sometimes he could go for two or three days hardly saying a word.

Finally, Brian walked out the front door for the last time as Carmen stood waving goodbye in the hallway.

The marriage had crumbled like the icing on his wedding cake. He and Sandra couldn't live together any more, and anyway it was better for Carmen if they didn't. The atmosphere was intolerable.

At first Carmen was withdrawn. She didn't understand what was going on and she really didn't want to. She just wanted to see her daddy. Her mother seemed happier but worried a lot, especially about money.

The couple divorced in 1971 and for the next five years Carmen saw her father once a month at her paternal grandparents' house. They were fun visits. Her father seemed happier and she would always come away with pocket money or presents. When she was older, Carmen told herself, she would find a man who would always stand by her, look after her. Marriage was for life, that's what the books said.

In 1976, when Carmen was eight years old, her mother Sandra remarried. Racing-car mechanic Kelvin Lambeth was a fun-loving and athletic-looking man with thick black hair and piercing brown eyes who owned two car showrooms in Essex. Cars were his passion. He drove an assortment of Ferraris and his old, metallic blue Dino Spyder was Carmen's favourite. But his relationship with Sandra was volatile. They fought like cat and dog. Carmen was desperately unhappy and took refuge in her schoolfriends. Her visits to her father Brian cheered her up, however, and over the years they were to become even closer. Often she would shut herself away in her bedroom. She loved to seclude herself there. She would take her favourite things with her to play in solitude and secrecy. It was her special place where she could escape when the world was too much for a little girl to handle. But Carmen was not prone to tears. She had grown up trying to be tough and strong.

Predictably though, Christmas was a difficult time. Her mother kept her busy cleaning the house and putting up the decorations. Carmen hung up her stocking, sang carols with friends but never went to church. Her mother had been brought up to believe in God, but she never did – and never would.

Even Christmas would sometimes be sad. For the rows between her mother and Kelvin grew more frequent and Carmen still missed her father terribly. Her mother, it seemed, was not lucky in her relationships.

When Carmen was ten the family moved to a rambling old house in Little Cambridge, near Great Dunmow in Essex. She took to the country straight away and loved the small farm next door with its smell of hay and freshly cut grass and the sounds of dogs and chickens and horses. Soon she was spending most of her spare time there and was almost a daughter to the owners Sarah and Alan Langford who didn't have any children. It was here that Carmen's great love of horses began.

By now the close ties between Carmen and her father were being broken, not least of all by geography. Her visits grew less frequent. Dunmow was a long way from Kettering, where her father now lived. Then came the news that her father had remarried a young receptionist named Marianne and on 6 April 1979 they had a son. Carmen hid her jealousy but it was hard. She had been close to her father, or thought she was, but now she wasn't his special little baby any more. That evening she wasn't celebrating. She lay fully dressed on her bed thinking about her life and listening to another row between her mother and Kelvin. Slowly their voices faded into a monotonous drone as her eyelids grew heavy and she finally fell asleep. When she woke, dawn was just beginning to break through the curtains. She turned over and buried her face in the pillow, trying to shut out the light of the day as well as the memory of yesterday. She tried to shut off the flow of sadness that threatened to engulf her. She felt hurt about her father's new child but was angry with herself. She was just being selfish, she reasoned. Her father would always love her. Carmen snapped herself out of her mood and got up. She looked out of the window across at the farm. That was where her future lay. Now she would throw herself even more into life with Sarah and Alan.

Her mother and stepfather seemed to understand Carmen's sense of isolation from her father and one bright, chilly May morning gave her the gift she would cherish for the rest of her schooldays – Cassie, a beautiful Palomino mare. From that day on, all Carmen's spare time was taken up with teaching herself equestrianism, She never had a single riding lesson: she just picked up the reins and took it from there. Her mother's secret little plan had worked. She had wanted Carmen to stop seeing her father and now Carmen was too absorbed in her new passion to think about the trips to Kettering.

She was busy practising for horse shows at nearby Finchingfield. She would get up at 5 a.m. on a Saturday morning and groom Cassie for the event. Then she and schoolfriend Andrea Reader would ride the seven miles from their homes to the competition, arriving at around 7.30 a.m., so that their horses had a rest before the show started. As they didn't have a horse-box they had to be sure their mounts were fit enough to compete. Carmen didn't win any of the events – but once proudly rode home clutching a blue ribbon for coming second.

Cassie, who appeared to have a scatty brain and a stubborn heart, turned out to be the best friend a girl could have. Carmen told her all her troubles. Life was good with Cassie, Sarah and Alan.

Cassie and Carmen only fell out once, while they were staying at her friend Andrea's house, which had two large stables about a mile down the road from Alan and Sarah's farm. Carmen was putting on her riding boots and didn't notice that the gate to the field was open. Cassie headed straight for it and disappeared in a cloud of gravel and dust. Carmen shouted herself hoarse, but it was no use. She walked home fuming to find Cassie resting and looking pleased with herself in Sarah's stables.

Summer was the time Carmen loved best. After Alan had harvested the field next to her house she would run out and roll the straw bales together then put sticks on the tops to make jumps for her and Cassie. Then they would spend hours each day practising. Sometimes Carmen would do a perfect round, sometimes she would fall in the hay, sometimes she would lie there on the ground dreaming she was at the Horse of the Year Show and the crowd was willing her to get to her feet.

In September 1979 Carmen started at the Helena Romanes School in Great Dunmow. There are bullies in all schools and Helena Romanes was no exception. As the winter months drew near Carmen grew more depressed. She was being picked on by a large, ungainly girl in the second year who had a reputation for being spiteful. All the younger girls were petrified of her, Carmen included. But she was determined to stand her ground. After all, even at twelve, she had taken enough knocks from life to understand that you just have to keep walking forward and face your problems – a trait that was to serve her well in the turbulent years to come.

One winter's afternoon in a corner of the playground the bully and her group of hangers-on approached Carmen and started to call her names. Then the girl began pushing and shoving her. Carmen kept her temper for a while but snapped when the bully clipped her around the ear. She turned and hit her back full in the face before pulling her to the ground. It was a ferocious fight. When they were pulled apart their faces were covered in blood. 'You hit hard,' the bully said, shaking. Carmen was never bullied again. But nothing comes easy. Carmen had broken a blood vessel in her nose and had to have it cauterised.

But there were fun times too. Fun and laughter with her best friend, classmate Emma Best. She and Carmen went everywhere together and were to forge a life-long friendship. Sometimes, however, there was sadness. Emma too had an unhappy home life, so they had a lot in common and leant on each other for support, something they were to do many times in the future.

They first met in a queue for the school tuck-shop. Carmen made a catty, schoolgirlish remark about Emma who was standing in front of her. Emma turned around and gave as good as she got. From that moment on they knew they were a match. The bond was formed. Emma found that Carmen wasn't an easy person to get to know. Often people did not understand her sense of humour. But under her tough exterior she was a very sensitive and caring person and fiercely loyal to her friends. There were no grey areas with her. She either liked someone or she didn't. It was all or nothing.

Carmen sometimes had the knack of being a devil in class and could create absolute mayhem. But when the moment dictated, she appeared to be the perfect angel. Often, when the teacher was at the end of his tether with the constant disturbances and peels of laughter coming from the back of the room, it was Emma who was sent outside to calm down.

The two were inseparable. Emma would spend the summer holidays at Carmen's house. Carmen's mother and Kelvin were mostly working all the time and so they had a free rein to do as they pleased. The neighbours all opened their houses to them – offering tennis courts, swimming pools and riding stables. There was no shortage of things to do.

When Carmen was sixteen she was like all girls of her age. Slowly horses were replaced by boys and she loved the feminine things in life like perfume and jewellery and trendy clothes. These were the whirlwind days of parties and clubbing all night, of pretending to be eighteen in the pub and skipping school. There wasn't enough time now to spend with Cassie and reluctantly she sold her, making sure she went to a good home – on a farm just a mile down the road.

One sticky September evening Carmen and her friend Emma were too hot to dance any more at the Barn disco in the village of Rayne near Braintree, Essex. They went outside, clutching their glasses of barley wine to get some fresh air, giggling and talking about the boys who had asked them to dance. They sat on the wall and laughed out loud, the drink going to their heads as passers-by smiled at them or simply ignored them. They both sipped their last sip of the treacly, black liquid and lost their balance in complete and utter unison. They laid there for some time on their backs, laughing hysterically with their feet in the air. All passers-by could see over the top of the wall were two pairs of ankles and platform heels.

The next day things weren't so funny at home where Emma was a guest for the weekend. Carmen and her mother had a fierce row, which was more or less a regular occurrence in these growing years when Carmen the girl was becoming Carmen the woman. Carmen stormed out with her bags packed and Emma in tow, vowing never to return. The two runaways got as far as the oak tree at the end of the road with Carmen still smarting.

'We'll hide here,' she announced to Emma, and they climbed the tree.

Half an hour later, Carmen's mother sped by on her way to Emma's house to round them up. Twenty minutes later, they watched from their tree-hideaway as she drove back again, worried sick. In her mind, Carmen wanted to teach her mother a lesson. The anger of the ups and downs and loneliness of her life was breaking through that morning. Two hours later, the runaways turned up on the doorstep. Tempers had subsided. There were tears and cuddles. Her mother laughed at the tale of the two monkeys in the tree.

But soon Carmen was to face another new beginning. Her mother and Kelvin had gone through one row too many and they got divorced. Carmen's father had moved back to Walthamstow with his family and, yearning for city life again, Carmen moved in with them. The only regret she had was leaving Emma. It was the end of an era.

It was Christmas 1984 and Carmen got a job waitressing at a pub in the City of London called the Bouncing Banker where she made many new friends before she left the following April. At last she was earning the sort of money that began to buy her freedom and independence.

But she missed her mother, who by now had typically jumped from the frying pan into the fire. She had gone on holiday to Mallorca and fallen in love with an Englishman named Paul Dyer who ran a bakery there. This was the fairytale love affair again, the man she had been waiting for all her life. Within months she was married and living in the sunshine.

Carmen, excited by the thought of sun, sea, sand and sangria went out to join them. For a while all went well, but then the rows began again. Carmen had seen the pattern before. Another of her mother's marriages was breaking down. Late one October morning, six months after she had fled to the sunshine, Carmen arrived back at Luton airport with her bags. She had left the sun, sangria and shouting behind and flown home to the peace and quiet of her father's house.

He had more news for her. He and Marianne were expecting their second child, but this time it didn't hurt Carmen as it had done before. She was eighteen later that month and planning her future. She felt strangely independent, sure of herself and she had one burning ambition – to travel the world. She wanted to drive across the plains of Africa, watch the sun rise over Bombay, see Lenin in his glass case in Moscow, lie on Australia's Bondi Beach. No, she didn't want to settle down and have babies yet. No, not until she was at least twenty-five.

Carmen went back to her old stamping grounds and was soon working again behind the bar at the Bouncing Banker pub. It was fun, all her friends were around and the money was good. Soon she was doing what all girls of eighteen do – going to discos, eating out and looking for clothes bargains in the markets.

Then, on the way home from work one evening, Carmen saw a familiar face. It was Emma. Unknown to either of them they had been working in the same London street for months. The bond was formed again.

Carmen rummaged through the blouses on the market stall in Petticoat Lane.

'I'm having a party for mum and dad at the weekend. It's their twenty-fifth. Do you fancy coming along?' asked her cousin Karen, picking up a bright yellow top and studying the label.

Karen's mother Pat was Carmen's father's sister.

They moved along to the record stall, where a young Asian lad in a denim shirt took off his sunglasses to admire Carmen's tan. She ignored him, but it made her feel good.

'I probably will, if I can get the time off from the pub,' she said, picking up a Rolling Stones album.

She looked for a moment at the group staring back at her from the record cover. She could never have guessed that one day one of them would become a family friend – in the most tragic of circumstances.

An hour later they walked back to the car, Carmen clutching two carrier bags stuffed with clothes and Karen trying on a headscarf, peeping at her reflection in the shop windows.

Carmen promised to try and come to the party at her cousin's house. It was a promise she kept and a party that changed her life. It was the sort of thing that only happened in movies and books. She was to see a man across a crowded room. They were to fall in love and exist suspended between two worlds. They were to talk, laugh and walk together. It was to be the beginning of Carmen's new tomorrow. A tomorrow tinged with sadness.

The sound of tinkling champagne glasses mingled with the sound of laughter. The DJ played Frank Sinatra's 'My Way' and Barry stared across the room at the pretty, bubbly blonde with the suntan talking to his auntie.

It was November 1985 and Barry had been back in London for almost a year, slipping in and out of relationships, never feeling strong enough to give all of himself and still holding on to what he had left back in LA. True, he was back at home living on the edge again, but that edge meant that every day he was just one step away from flying back to America. The truth was that as soon as he had stepped back on English soil he felt he had made the wrong decision. Only his family, the clan, helped him through and especially his cousin Pete. Barry realised he had missed that feeling of honesty and true friendship through blood relations – something he could never have in America. He had missed, too, the things he had once taken for granted – rummaging through cabbages in Alf's greengrocer shop, playing darts at the local pub, a pint of milk delivered to the doorstep, a flutter on the Grand National.

Auntie Pat's 25th wedding anniversary party was a family affair. Barry slowly made his way around cousin Karen's front room until he ended up beside the girl with the suntan who was talking about the beaches in Mallorca to Karen's husband Steve. Soon Barry was talking about beaches with them too and about sunshine and about hot days and about deserts and Indians and America and music and . . . Steve was called away to pour more beers.

Carmen discovered Barry worked for a record and video distribution network in the East End called Gold's. He discovered she worked in a pub in the City. She found out he played the guitar. He found out she loved horses. He talked about his family, the clan, but mostly about his father. She talked about her family, the stepfathers, but mostly about her mother. They both forgot about the party. He wanted to be in a quiet place, just with her. But did she really like him? He was much older, and she was so young, bubbly and beautiful. She wanted to see him again: they seemed to just click. But would he ask her out?

'What's wrong, Dad?' asked Barry.

His father walked across to the fireplace and stood in the corner next to his stash — the little sacred area in the lounge where he had kept his books and knick-knacks for over thirty years. 'I haven't told your mother yet, son, but I've got cancer and they say there's not much hope.'

His words were a bombshell. Barry stopped strumming his guitar on the sofa and the sound of his last chord seemed to float around the room for ever. It was all so unfair. His father had only been retired a year or so. He had worked so hard all of his life and now . . . and now this.

Barry didn't know what to say. Just when his father was getting some time to himself fate was taking it away from him. Barry wondered if his five-year stay in America had anything to do with the illness. He felt guilty. He knew his parents had missed him terribly and worried about him the whole time. This was clan country. Family and friends. A bonding. But he had broken that bond. Perhaps the pressure on his parents was the trigger that had ruined his father's health.

Barry had only been home a few weeks and was settling back into the family way of life. Now his father stood in front of him holding a piece of paper with the time of his chemotherapy appointment on it. He had cancer of the oesophagus. Barry put down his guitar and stood hugging his father by the fireplace. Father and son bonded for eternity.

Barry parked his brown and black Audi GT outside number 22 in the road of restored Victorian houses. Carmen came down the path looking absolutely stunning. Her suntanned skin and blonde hair complementing the gold necklace and shimmering white dress. He was so glad he had managed to invite her out. It had been six weeks since his auntie's anniversary party. He just hadn't been able to pluck up the courage before. But now he needed something, someone, to help him cope with the sadness he felt over his father.

The steak sizzled on the plate, nestling against the green peppers and onions and tomatoes and French fries as the red-haired waitress poured the *béarnaise* sauce from a silver jug. The four of them – he and Carmen, cousin Karen and her husband Steve – talked and laughed and drank Chablis and bottles of beer at the Colorado Exchange in Buckhurst Hill, Essex. Life was free and easy. Barry loved the company of his cousin Karen and her husband Steve. Karen was his Uncle Brian's daughter. Uncle Brian was his mother's brother and he was married to Pat, Carmen's father's sister. This, again, was clan country. Something Barry felt comfortable with. But he couldn't help feeling there was something special about Carmen and Carmen couldn't help feeling there was something special about Barry. They wanted to be together. The time would come, somehow they both knew that in their own way.

Barry dropped Carmen off at her father's house. The lights were still on, and he didn't really want to go inside. He kissed her goodnight and the musical dream of America faded like the last chord of a David Bowie song.

On a bright, clear Saturday morning three days later, Carmen pushed and squeezed her way through the bustling crowds at Walthamstow market, stopping here and there to look at a skirt or a top, a pair of trousers or a pair of shoes.

Nothing was good enough and the hours ticked by. There was no time for a bacon roll, a hot dog or even a coffee at Joe's burger van. She desperately needed something stylish, something new that she felt good in, something . . . something Barry would find sexy.

At 8.00 that evening she and Barry arrived at the Chingford Assembly Hall for Auntie Josie's annual company Christmas dinner.

Barry couldn't take his eyes off Carmen. The pretty blonde in the silky black trouser suit and patent black shoes with her shiny, matching handbag looked like a million dollars. Heads turned in the hall, but not because they looked such a trendy, well-suited couple. It was because everyone expected Barry to arrive with Juicy Lucy – a young vivacious redhead he had been seen around town with.

As the weeks went by Carmen and Barry became closer. They listened to Gino Vanelli's *Brother to Brother* album over and over, lying by the fireside. Barry had brought it back with him from America and it conjured up memories of the South Dakota dust, the cattle markets, the neon lights of Las Vegas, the dreams and hopes of Hollywood – and the face of his father not wanting him to take the lonesome trail across the Atlantic with just a kitbag, a guitar and a fistful of dollars.

There were wild weekends with Karen and Steve, discoing, clubbing, pubbing. But there were homely weekends too – staying at Karen and Steve's house playing board games, Trivial Pursuit or Pictionary, and cooking chilli and laughing themselves to sleep in front of old *Carry On* movies.

'I'm afraid Mr Daniels will die quite soon. His only chance is an operation.'

The doctor's words echoed in Barry's ears. He turned and looked at his mother sitting motionless in the chair and staring at the floor with tears in her eyes. Then he looked at his brother David who seemed to be in a lost world.

It was a chilly March afternoon in 1986 and Barry gazed, glassy-eyed, out of the window of the little consulting room in St Margaret's Hospital, where he had once lain on a bed in a coma as his father sat by his side night and day. Now the roles were reversed and Barry vowed to himself he would be as strong as his father had been in his hour of need.

'What are his chances of coming through the operation?' he asked.

'Well, there are always problems with surgery, especially in dealing with something like this,' the doctor answered solemnly. 'Perhaps it is something you should discuss with your father.'

Later they sat around his bed in the long, airy ward, Barry, David and their mother. None of them really knew what to do. Of one thing Barry was sure: he desperately wanted his father to live and he had to give him every fighting chance.

'You've got to do it, dad. You've got to have the surgery,' he said.

His father was his greatest mentor. He was just a wonderful man, everyone thought so. He had worked so hard all of his life, and for what? To end up like this. Life just wasn't fair. Barry remembered his younger days. Dad would work all week at County Hall, then earn extra money for them in the accounts department at the Crystal Palace motor-racing track at the weekends.

When he finally retired at 63, his garden became his life. If Barry's mother couldn't find him, she would make her way down to the greenhouse where he would be sitting on a chair among his plants.

When Barry had returned home in December 1984, after five years in America, he brought with him the memory of his broken relationship with Ginny. He was shattered, confused, hurt and tormented. He had brought those feelings into the front room of his parents' home. Did his distress affect his father? His father, after all, had always felt his pain.

Then one year on, his life had begun to come together. Time was a great healer. But as Barry grew stronger, his father grew weaker and for the next six months he was in and out of hospital.

Barry was consumed with guilt that he had brought on his father's illness, although the consultants told him it wasn't true. He hated seeing his father lying in bed all the time, losing weight and not being able to eat. He should have been in the greenhouse, pottering around the kitchen or getting most of the questions right watching yet another TV quiz programme and putting the rest of the family to shame because they had the wrong answers. Now it seemed like he was just waiting to die.

Only Carmen was getting Barry through. She had captured his heart . . . and his mind. He didn't know, didn't understand why she seemed to like him so much. He felt so uninteresting, so preoccupied with his father's illness. Even his music was blue.

They sat holding hands and joking and talking about rings, the flickering candle on the table throwing a warm glow across their brandy glasses, the soft music dulling their senses along with the two bottles of wine they had already consumed.

It wasn't crowded at Topo Gigio's Italian restaurant in London's West End that night, although it was only a week before Christmas. Carmen loved being wined and dined, and the last few months of going out with Barry had been a whole new experience for her. He was the first man who had ever treated her like a special person.

It was strange how the conversation got on to rings. They sat trying on each other's, looking at them in the candlelight, holding each other's fingers.

Seven days later Carmen got a very special Christmas present from Barry – a three-stone sapphire and diamond ring. She vowed to wear it on her middle finger for the rest of her life.

Barry picked up the telephone. It was 2 April 1986 and he had received the call he had prayed he would never get.

'Mr Daniels?'

'Yes.'

'Please come to the hospital immediately to see your father.'

'Is he all right?'

'The doctor will speak to you when you get here.

I'm afraid that's all I can say.'

Barry drove his mother to the hospital not really knowing what to expect. All he knew was that he had to get to his father's side. He felt a shambles. He was unshaven and hastily dressed in old, faded, tracksuit trousers and a T-shirt. His mind was in a shambles . . . and the hospital was a shambles too.

His father was in a ward with about ten other patients. A curtain had been pulled around his bed. Barry didn't need to be told where his father was, he could hear his screams. His father was in agony. He needed him as he so often had needed his father in his life.

'Why have you bloody well left him like that?' he shouted at the junior houseman.

Barry gripped his struggling father's arm to try and keep him steady and then turned again on the doctors. He just couldn't believe they would leave his father in that state, they just didn't seem to have any concern for the pain he was suffering.

Barry was shouting and the ward was in uproar.

'I want something done, something done now!'

His distressed mother broke down in tears as they were both ushered into a side room.

'Mr Daniels, your father is still under the anaesthetic. He doesn't know what he is doing or where he is.'

It was difficult to calm Barry down. This was his father. How dare they treat him like that, like a number. This was the man who had taught him to play cricket, been by his side in every crisis, nursed him when he was sick and felt his hurt. Now he needed him and Barry would be there no matter what the consequences.

But the stress was too much for him. He was

overwhelmed with emotion and burst into tears.

'Where's David? Why isn't David here?' he blurted out.

His mother sat on the chair not saying anything. The doctor and two nurses in the room stood quietly watching him. He brushed the tears from his eyes and took a deep breath. His brother was away on business somewhere and Barry really wanted his support. He didn't want to go through this without him. That fact angered him somehow.

They sat Barry down and the doctor's voice broke the new silence.

'We can give your father something to calm him, to take away his pain,' he said.

Barry looked at him, wondering why his voice was so calm and clipped, so matter-of-fact.

'I'm afraid the surgery hasn't worked. The cancer is everywhere.'

An hour later Barry stood in silence staring down at the body of the man who had meant more to him than life itself. He looked so peaceful, as if all his troubles and pain had been taken away by the hand of God.

Barry didn't know, even at that moment, how hard his father's death would hit him.

David arrived at the house as soon as he could get there. His mother's brothers arrived and Barry walked around pouring cups of tea or glasses of brandy or gin without really listening to what people were saying. Nothing had prepared him for the way he was feeling. Death may have been a servant to his father but it was an evil intruder into Barry's life.

When Carmen arrived, her blonde hair tumbling over her cheeks and her eyes so deeply sympathetic, his face lit up. He was as smitten now as he had always been by her pretty looks and her air of intrinsic kindness. He had always seen her as a cut above himself, an almost fairytale girl who reminded him of the illustration in a book he had read as a boy. The kind of woman a white knight would slay dragons for.

Little did he know then how much they would need each other's firm and comforting support in the years ahead.

Barry had never been a religious kind of person, but he had always believed in God and had gone to church on the big occasions, at Easter, Christmas and harvest festival.

But on a grey, rainy morning a few days later, he sat in St John's Church, a short walk from his home, trying to understand his father's illness and death. He asked God the questions that grieving sons do. With all the evil people in the world, the rapists, the baby killers, the terrorists who bomb children and their peace-loving families without a thought, why take this good, kind, caring man? But Barry didn't feel he was getting any answers back.

He was to sit in that same church a few years later telling God just what he thought about him.

The funeral service and cremation of his father was unbearable for Barry. The whole clan was there and came back to the house and cheered him up some-how. The day became one of celebration for the life of his father, the happy memories, a toast to a super human being. Barry stood in the hall with Carmen and held her close. He needed her like he had never needed anyone before.

For two weeks Barry struggled to come to terms with reality. Carmen moved into his parents' home, to help him through the bad times. He lost himself in the world of his guitar and sad songs. Carmen just sat listening.

That summer they got engaged and took their first holiday together in Rimini, in Italy. It was to be a new beginning. Barry felt as if his troubles and feelings of despair had been left in another world. The mornings were spent lying on the sloping beaches that were ringed by clean promenades and towering hotels. In the afternoons they wandered around parts of the ancient city in the footsteps of Michelangelo, Shelley and D. H. Lawrence and in the evenings they dined on grilled mushrooms, risotto, pasta and wine.

Barry loved the food shops with their huge sacks of cereals and fruit and tables stacked with gorgonzola cheese, the smell of the railway repair warehouses and the bobbing, millionaires' yachts in the marina that wound its way out to the Adriatic. They drank coffee in the railway station watching the world go by as people arrived from Brindisi, Venice, Trieste, Bologna and Turin.

The break did Barry a power of good and when they returned he felt ready to get on with life. They decided to buy a flat, for by now Barry's mother seemed strong enough to cope on her own. She had lived in Epping for 25 years and she had many friends around her, not forgetting the clan.

By the autumn Barry and Carmen were soon firmly ensconced in a little two-bedroom home in east London.

Their relationship grew even stronger and arguments were few – until Barry went to find his long-lost and dearly missed friend Chris Sutton, whom he had not seen for over six years.

Chris was rehearsing with his new group at Blackboard Studios in south London. They were about to go on a UK tour to support his debut album.

Barry turned up at the studio and the two of them

were overjoyed to see each other. They hugged each other in front of the band and later in front of a barman in a nearby pub. Then, many beers and a few joints later, Barry managed to stagger home. Carmen had never seen him in such a state.

Barry needed to do some damage limitation. The following weekend he took Carmen to see singer George Benson at the Wembley Arena. A good move. Peace was restored. Meanwhile they put a lot of hard work into their flat and redecorated every room to their taste. Their own home at last. But they didn't stay there long. The family house was too big for Barry's mother to run and so he and Carmen moved back in and bought it from the council.

Carmen looked out of the window at the beautiful, clear, crisp, sunny morning. It was 7.30 a.m. on Saturday, 26 September 1987 – her wedding day. She had stayed the night at her cousin Karen's house in Walthamstow and Karen had manicured and painted her nails for the big occasion.

At 8.30 a.m. the make-up woman from the cosmetics shop arrived. Carmen was fussy. She didn't want to wear too much; she hated anything that was over the top. She didn't even want to be married in a church – Epping registry office was fine with her. She just liked the simple things. The bouquets arrived and she thought they looked rather pretty considering she wasn't very fond of flowers. She had wanted to wear a red suit for the occasion but Karen and her mother had bullied her into wearing a white wedding dress, with a pearl necklace and lace tiara. Karen sat beside her in the car on the way to the registry office and they both had a good swear to steady their nerves.

As the car turned the corner, Carmen could see

Barry standing outside the registrar's office resplendent in a purple suit, white shirt and pink and green tie.

'Good job I didn't wear that red suit after all,' she said to Karen.

'Trust Barry,' Karen replied. 'He just doesn't want to look ordinary. It's a wonder he hasn't dyed his hair some weird colour to match his suit!'

The service went without a hitch. All the clan was there. Barry's brother David was the best man and he lent the happy couple his posh, black BMW car for the trip back to the house, where the champagne and beer flowed.

At 7.30 p.m. that evening everyone arrived for the bash at St Patrick's Hall in Walthamstow. The clan had arranged everything, even the huge buffet of cold meats, baked potatoes and pies. The hall was packed when Barry had his little joke ... requesting a song that was very special to Carmen. The disc jockey played Frank Sinatra's 'Summer Breeze'. Carmen never could stand Old Blue Eyes and always turned him down when Barry played him on the stereo.

When it was time to go Barry and Carmen said goodbye to everyone in the hall, jumped in a taxi and sped off to a secret, romantic destination. No one had a clue where they were off to. Some said America, others thought Spain. In fact, they spent the night at the Ridgeway Hotel in Chingford, Essex. The next morning they were told there was a 45-minute wait for a taxi, so they rang Carmen's father Brian, who lived just ten minutes away. Flabbergasted, he picked them up and took them home.

'Keep very still,' said the nurse.

'But I'm having bloody contractions!' Carmen

shouted back, gritting her teeth as the needle went into her spine.

'There now, soon you won't feel a thing.'

Carmen felt herself going numb from the middle of her body downwards. Barry was holding her hand, speaking to her in muffled tones from behind his surgical mask.

It was around 4 a.m. on Saturday, 23 April 1988 and Carmen was giving birth.

It had been a long, hard nine months during which time she had put on over five stone in weight. On 21 April, the day the baby was due, Carmen had gone for an antenatal check-up at the hospital. The doctor was worried about her blood pressure and decided the baby might have to be induced. He booked her in for the next day.

But nature began to take its course and the following morning the contractions began. Barry drove his wife to Whipps Cross Hospital, east London, worrying all the way as fathers-to-be do.

The midwife wasn't happy. Carmen didn't seem to be coping too well. She was given gas and air and Pethidine in the delivery suite and the contractions began to slow down. The hours ticked by until around 4 a.m. on Saturday, 23 April, when the doctor decided enough was enough. He told Carmen to prepare herself for an emergency Caesarean and Barry changed into a surgical gown.

As she lay in the operating theatre feeling her spine go numb from the injection, she began not to care about what was happening. The doctor said he was going to try a forceps delivery, but his words didn't really sink in. There was no pain, she was sort of floating.

'All you will feel will be a bit of tugging,' the doctor reassured her.

The midwife felt for contractions and the forceps were placed on the baby's head. There was just one big pull and she was out.

Little Charlotte Elisabeth Georgina Daniels weighed into the world at 7 lb 10 oz.

'Doesn't she look like Nan!' Carmen blurted out. She was just glad it was all over, that her baby was all right. The perfect child.

Carmen had always hated cereals but that morning she gobbled down two bowls of cornflakes. It was one of the best meals she had ever had in her life. Then the clan began to arrive. Everyone agreed, Charly was a beautiful baby.

She was christened on Sunday, 11 September at St Mary's Church in Woodford. She looked beautiful in her christening gown and bonnet, just like a little doll. Her godparents were Carmen's cousin Karen, her former schoolfriend Sue and Barry's brother David. Barry and Carmen counted their blessings.

4: Charly Girl

Charly's looks impressed the modelling agencies. Her wide-eyed innocence, long blonde hair and natural beauty were a joy to behold. Carmen dreamed of her daughter being on the catwalk in Milan. Barry dreamed of her one day marrying a millionaire rock star. Now she had a contract to model for Trotters, the new children's wear chain.

The woman who had made and lost a fortune selling socks had been inspired by her own bored children to seek success again. Sophie Mirman had hit on the idea for a revolutionary new children's clothes store when she saw how her youngsters hated shopping trips. There was nothing worse than a bored child when they were out with mum and dad shopping. She decided there and then to open a special tot shop that would be fun for the kids. And she needed very special kids to model for her.

The first branch of Dunwoody 'n' Trotter was opening in London's King's Road within a few weeks. Sophie's dream was that it would do for busy mothers what Sock Shop did for working women.

The whole purpose was to make shopping for clothes fun for both parents and children.

73

Sophie had plans to bring in clowns and magicians to entertain the youngsters. They would be able to drink fruit juice at a bar built like a factory, watch cartoons in a video corner, have their hair cut on a mock ocean liner and try on shoes while sitting in a model steam train.

At the same time, mothers would be able to kit out their children with the latest fashions from Clarks, Start Rite, Buckle My Shoe, Kickers and Dr Martens.

Sophie, 33, a former Marks and Spencer assistant and Businesswoman of the Year, was determined to make things work. Everything had to be just right. Her Sock Shops empire had collapsed the previous summer and she could never forget the message from the bank that an administrator should be brought in to run the business she had struggled so hard to build from nothing. This time though, this time, she wouldn't go wrong.

Sock Shop had slumped disastrously from a market high of £70 million to be sold finally for just £3.25 million. Sophie was left with nothing to show for her 80 per cent stake and a decade of devotion to a retail dream that came to embody Premier Margaret Thatcher's new Britain.

Sophie loved the modelling agency's pictures of Charly. She was bang on the image she wanted to project. Clothes in her new store were to be casual but smart. Osh Kosh dungarees would take their place on the shelves beside Levi 501 jeans and Mexx bomber jackets. They had to be quality clothes that could be passed down from one child to the next.

'Let's have a look at her,' Sophie said to her husband Richard. He passed her the photographs. 'Yes, she looks perfect,' he said.

On Monday, 15 October 1990, Charly appeared in

the *Today* newspaper modelling Sophie's dream in front of the toy steam engine in her new store. Barry and Carmen were so proud, so confident of the future. Where would it all end?

'Up you get, Charly!' Barry got his daughter to her feet. She had tripped over again.

'She must be the clumsiest little girl in Epping,' said Carmen.

Charly was always bumping into things, or falling over. But she had no fear, always picking herself up again and carrying on. They watched her climb the steps to the slide. She got near the top and almost fell, steadying herself on the handrail. Barry rushed over and stood at the foot of the steps just in case.

The next day they arrived at the Russell Hotel in London's Russell Square for the modelling audition for Peaudouce nappies. The ballroom was full of screaming children and parents shouting commands, brushing long, flowing locks of hair and polishing little shoes with hankies. Charly was withdrawn and quiet. The noise was all too much for her.

'Let's forget it,' said Carmen.

Barry looked at Charly who was staring across the room. 'OK, let's go.'

That evening at home Barry tried to get Charly to watch the children's cartoons on TV but she just wouldn't concentrate on them. But then, she never did like TV much, or books. She would pick a book up, look at the pictures for a minute, then wander off. Every time he began to read to her she would get off his lap and do something else.

'You really have the attention span of a butterfly,' he would joke.

*   *   *

It was a hot August evening when Barry's brother David rang and asked him if he could get a team together to install computerised-locking systems for his company in Strasbourg, France.

'Cousin Pete will be up for it,' said Barry. 'And Uncle John and Brian are out of work.'

The four of them were soon ensconced in the luxury of the Strasbourg Hilton for ten days. They worked hard and partied hard. When the hotel bar closed in the wee small hours Pete and Barry would hit the town, just like they used to when they worked at the old Atherfield Bay holiday camp on the Isle of Wight.

It was just a one-off job, but they did it so well, even with the hangovers, that they were offered a permanent contract. When they returned home they formed a company, Teamacre Limited. It was a very apt name as they really were a tremendous team. Pete was the only one not to join the others. He was off to become a catering manager for Grand Metropolitan hotels.

'Where's the labour ward?' Carmen screamed at the nurse, as she and Barry rushed into the hospital.

'That way,' she said, pointing to her right.

They hurried down the corridor as Carmen clutched her stomach.

The excruciating cramp had started that morning when she got up. It had got so bad as she was brushing Charly's hair that she rang the Princess Alexandra Hospital in Harlow, Essex, and they told her to come straight in. Barry had driven like a lunatic and at one stage she thought she would end up in casualty and not the maternity wing.

At 10.00 that morning, Friday, 28 December 1990,

Carmen was wheeled into the delivery suite. She was allowed gas and air and nothing else.

'We'll have this baby out by 10.30,' said the midwife.

Carmen started to push.

'Don't forget to breathe,' the midwife added.

'I suppose it would help!' said Carmen, trying to make a joke of things.

At 10.32 little Rhys William Daniels popped into the world, a healthy 8 lb 1 oz.

Barry and Carmen could hardly believe their good fortune. They had one of each, a boy and a girl. Their family was complete. But Carmen would not have been at all bothered if Rhys had turned out to be a girl. She got so much enjoyment out of Charly. They both did.

Life was idyllic. Barry didn't mind getting up in the middle of the night to feed his baby son. He would switch on CNN and watch the Gulf War coverage, making himself a cup of tea. Little did he know then that some three years later he would be working in the Tel Aviv Hilton, where the balcony in his room still bore the scars of the blast from a Scud missile, courtesy of Saddam Hussein.

Barry and his uncles John and Brian Alderman were now working full-time for Teamacre Limited. Their first big job was a three-week trip to refit the Amsterdam Hilton. Barry hated leaving his family but the travelling man in him was getting a feel for the work – and the money was good. The highlight of the mission was Barry having his picture taken in the John Lennon suite. Once again the rock-star flame in him could not be stubbed out.

Rhys was christened at St John's Church in Epping on Sunday, 28 April 1991. His godparents were Barry's brother David and his girlfriend Carolyn, who was soon to be his wife, and Carmen's cousin Marvin. Once again the whole clan gathered back at the house as it was a joint party for Charly's third birthday as well. But she seemed very bewildered and quiet.

'Is she OK?' Barry asked.

'Well, she doesn't seem her normal self. Perhaps it's all the excitement,' Carmen answered.

They both stared over at her.

Charly just sat quietly in the corner not wanting to play with her cousins. They were worried about her. Minutes later Charly walked towards her father staring at him and he put his arms out to her . . . but she just walked by in a world of her own.

'My God, she's dead!' Barry almost threw himself at the chair. Charly was slumped across it with her eyes wide open. He grabbed her arm and felt her pulse and quickly put his fingers to her little nose. She was alive – but barely breathing.

It was 4.30 p.m. on Friday, 22 March 1991, a day firmly embedded in the history of the Daniels family.

Carmen was standing at the front door chatting to her neighbour Christine when Barry arrived home from work with his two uncles, John and Brian. Tired and in need of a shower he said a polite hello to Christine, kissed Carmen on the cheek and went in.

It was as if a knife had been thrust into his stomach as he walked into the lounge and saw Charly lifeless in the chair.

Minutes later he had scooped her up in his arms and shouted to his two uncles who were sitting in the old blue Ford Escort talking to Carmen and Christine.

Barry lay Charly, still wide-eyed and staring vacantly, on the lounge floor and Uncle John, who had some first-aid knowledge, tried to bring her round. Suddenly Charly coughed.

'Thank God,' said Carmen, gripping Barry's arm as they watched helplessly. Slowly, Charly got her senses back and everything seemed OK. What on earth could have been wrong with her?

Barry sat with his daughter on the sofa, stroking her hair as Carmen made some tea. He wondered if she had some kind of virus, but she didn't seem to have a high temperature. Then she suffered another bad turn. Her head fell back and she began to drift in and out of consciousness.

Carmen rang for an ambulance. Was Charly dying? She and Barry put the thought from their minds. But they knew this was serious.

Barry threw the cup across the kitchen and it shattered on the wall.

'Where the bloody hell are they?' he shouted.

'Ring again,' Carmen screamed back from the lounge as she sat on the sofa cuddling Charly who was staring vacantly at the ceiling. Rhys cried. He hated the sound of his father shouting. Barry picked up his son and cuddled him before handing him over to his own mother who had arrived to have Rhys for the night. Then he rang for the ambulance again.

'Look, this is bloody well urgent. My daughter could be dying for all I know!'

Finally, after 25 minutes, which seemed like hours, the ambulance arrived.

At St Margaret's Hospital the two doctors were baffled. Their tests didn't show up any abnormalities, but the little girl with flowing blonde hair and haunting blue eyes was obviously seriously ill. There was nothing more they could do. They would have to send her for more tests at a hospital with special equipment.

Within hours Barry, Carmen and Charly were on their way in an ambulance to the Princess Alexandra Hospital in Harlow, where there were more bemused doctors. Poor Charly hated having needles stuck in her. Her sugar levels were tested, she underwent a lumbar puncture and an ECG. Nothing was wrong.

The next evening in the hospital ward, she seemed fine, as bright as a button. They all sat around the bed laughing and joking. Barry kissed her on the cheek and Carmen unpacked the little pink and blue dress she had brought her from home. The mystery virus had gone. It was just one of those things. The doctors said she could have just fainted. Barry and Carmen hoped they were right.

They all sat in the lounge: Barry, Carmen, her father Brian and his wife Marianne and their children. Rhys was in his cot and Charly was generally running around.

Barry and Carmen were drinking glasses of wine and flicking through tour brochures, talking about going to Lanzarote in the Canaries for a holiday. They desperately needed a break.

Suddenly Charly ran towards Barry shouting: 'Daddy, daddy!'

'Yes, Charly?' said Barry, looking up from the pictures of the shimmering blue swimming pools and restaurants.

Charly was looking over his shoulder at the wall. She was calling to him but she couldn't see him, just like before.

Barry shouted to Carmen, a couple of feet away. He grabbed Charly as she fell and she was sick all over him.

At nearby Whipps Cross Hospital, doctors told

them that Charly had suffered an epileptic fit. There was nothing they could do for her. They were referred to their local doctor for anti-convulsant medicines and advised to read up on how to deal with the condition at home.

Barry and Carmen drove back to Epping with mixed feelings. Relief that it must have been a fit that caused the collapse at home two weeks earlier and anxiety that they had to learn how to deal with epilepsy. Still they could handle that. It wasn't the end of the world for them – or her. Lots of people had epilepsy. Thousands even. Hundreds of thousands. Millions. Barry borrowed books on the condition from the local library.

A string of medical appointments followed over the next few months and by the end of May that year Charly was being treated for the condition.

Then things began to go from bad to worse. None of the drugs were helping her. Charly started to have problems walking and within two weeks she could hardly stand on her feet. She was also having 'drop attacks', losing all sense of balance and falling from the chair to the floor. Barry and Carmen's nerves were shattered as they tried to live their lives near her, so that they could catch her if she fell. Her head was bruised and her lips and cheeks bore the scars of cut after cut.

'For God's sake, why can't she just lie down and she won't hurt herself,' Barry screamed at Carmen one night. He didn't mean it. It was just frustration. But Charly wouldn't sit down. She had no fear, she wanted to run and play and do all the normal things that children do.

The doctors suspected that she was reacting to the strong drugs prescribed for epilepsy. Barry demanded that more was done. His GP, Dr Diane Lowry, was sympathetic and concerned and referred Barry and Carmen to Great Ormond Street for more tests under Dr John Wilson who immediately changed Charly's treatment.

Over the following few weeks, Charly's walking improved, although she was still very unstable and in need of constant supervision.

Barry sat on the crowded plane staring out of the window. He couldn't eat the airline breakfast and he put the blue tin-foil lid back over the half-eaten sausage and scrambled egg. He had been on too many trips abroad already that year and spent hundreds of pounds telephoning to see how Charly was. He wanted to be with his family – but he also had to keep working. Now he had to get home quickly. Charly was going into Great Ormond Street that afternoon to begin three days of extensive diagnostic tests.

'Good morning everyone. This is your pilot, Captain David Sinclair, speaking. We are cruising quite comfortably at around 30,000 feet. Coming up on your right is the Polish border and soon we will be heading out over the Baltic, then down the European coastline to France, a short hop over the Channel to the White Cliffs of Dover and on to Stansted.

'Weather reports are, well, not too encouraging. A lot of ground fog at the airport, but let's hope it will clear within the next hour or so. Meanwhile enjoy your breakfast and I'll be back with an update on that fog as soon as I get a clearer picture.'

Barry's stomach turned over. He was two hours late already. Why did airline pilots always sound so bloody cool?

It was 2 February 1992, and Barry had been working in Romania.

A month earlier he had agreed with his company that he should move off managing the installation team and go on to the computer-training side. It seemd a good idea and meant only being away for up to five days at a time. No more three-week trips. Romania was the last installation job. He had been based at the Intercontinental hotel in Bucharest, so he had been cushioned from the real world of deprivation in the country. During the day he would walk by the long lines of people who queued for hours for just one loaf of bread. There were black market deals going on everywhere and at night the bars in all the hotels were lined with prostitutes plying for trade with businessmen from all over the world.

The flight from Bucharest to London had already been delayed and now Barry was worried that Stansted would be fogbound and the plane wouldn't be able to land. Carmen had brought Charly with her and driven down to Stansted to meet him. He had tried to get through to her on the telephone from Bucharest airport to warn her of the hold-up, but no joy.

His worst fears materialised. The fog was causing chaos and the plane was diverted to Birmingham. It was sod's law on the very day his family needed him most. He felt the fist of anger punching away inside him. Suddenly he didn't feel like living on the edge any more.

Barry sat on the coach outside the glass and steel airport concourse in Birmingham watching the packed monorail train wind its way around the concrete sky road into the railway station. The coach journey down the M6 to London and then on to Stansted was the longest journey he had ever taken.

Carmen was tired when she met him. Tired with worry and waiting and driving. Barry hugged and kissed Charly reassuringly and tried to apologise to Carmen, but they didn't speak much in the car. They didn't have to. They knew what they meant to say to each other. Barry cracked a joke. It wasn't much of a joke, but she laughed, half not hearing. He put his hand on her knee.

'It'll be all right, love,' he said.

She nodded, wanting to believe him.

They stayed at the hospital for two nights and three days, sometimes sleeping in a little side room, sometimes dozing off by Charly's side, sometimes making telephone calls to see how Rhys was, sometimes just walking in the grounds.

Finally, the tests were done and they were on their way home in the car, through London's East End and their old Walthamstow stomping ground and out down the A11 to the bare, winter trees of Epping Forest. They had been told to take Charly home and to return without her on Friday for the results of the tests.

'Without her,' said Carmen. 'They told us to go back without her.'

'That doesn't mean anything,' said Barry. 'If it was anything really serious they would have kept her in.'

Carmen was frightened, bloody frightened, as she sat in the back of the car cuddling Charly. She feared the worst. But she took heart in Barry's optimism.

'Everything is going to be OK,' he said to Carmen looking at her face in the windscreen mirror for a few moments. How wrong could he be?

On the day of their appointment, they were quietly led into Dr John Wilson's small office with its bar charts and no-smoking sign. As soon as the door closed behind them they knew something was badly wrong. Dr Wilson cleared his throat.

'I'm sorry, but I have some really bad news for you,' he said. Barry and Carmen didn't say anything. They just sat waiting, they didn't know what for. Was it cancer? Leukaemia? Both diseases could be treated, Barry quickly reasoned with himself.

'Charly is suffering from Batten's disease and she will deteriorate rapidly over the next few years.'

Barry and Carmen were dumbstruck.

'What is Batten's disease?' Barry choked on the words.

The doctor was so matter-of-fact.

'It is a devastating genetic, neurological, degenerative disease that affects people of all ages, but especially infants, toddlers and school-age children,' he said, looking Barry straight in the eye.

'It begins unexpectedly and leads to early death. There are four types. With the late infantile form, outlined by medical experts Jansky and Bielschowsky some years ago, children usually die by the age of ten. Charly has late infantile.'

Barry and Carmen were struggling with the reality of it all. The strange names, the diagnosis. They hadn't in their wildest dreams expected any of this.

The words echoed in their ears. It was an inherited disorder primarily affecting the brain and vision, leading to a progressive loss of brain function.

The doctor turned and tapped the chart of the human body on the wall behind him. It was like being snapped out of a hypnotic trance.

'Acting through the nervous system, this disease destroys all other body functions as well, leaving the child helpless.'

He turned to face them again.

'What causes it?' Carmen blurted out. 'Why can't it be cured?'

'The specific reasons for the loss in brain functions are not known. We still have very little understanding of the real cause or biochemical mechanism involved in Batten's disease. We don't know enough to do anything about it.'

'How do you know Charly really has it?' asked Barry, hoping against hope that there would still be a chance it was all a big mistake.

'Well, with the advancement in medical technology, diagnosis is becoming much more refined, especially for rare conditions such as this,' he said, almost apologetically.

'Early symptoms of Batten's disease are confusing. Often it begins with overt changes in personality and behaviour and a decline in learning ability. Clumsiness, stumbling and failing vision soon follow. Most patients have seizures, rather like epilepsy. The child or adult deteriorates progressively. Motor co-ordination is lost, blindness develops, mental changes become severe and seizures become more frequent. These changes are particularly devastating in young children who have just begun to experience life. Their decline is often quite sudden. Four types of Batten's disease have been identified based on age of onset and the severity of the symptoms. They are infantile, late infantile, juvenile and adult. Charly has all the symptoms of late infantile. Do you want me to go on?'

Barry and Carmen both quietly nodded.

'Just how specific would you like me to be?'

'We've got to know everything,' said Barry.

'Very well. The order of specific symptoms varies with each type. The infantile type has an onset at around the age of one to two with seizures and rapid deterioration and death by the age of six. Late infantile disease strikes toddlers like Charly at three to four years of age with death by ten.'

The doctor paused for a moment.

'Please go on,' said Barry.

'Juveniles may live with blindness, seizures and mental retardation until their early twenties, while the rarer adult form, beginning in early adulthood, progresses more slowly.

'For example, juvenile Batten's disease victims lose their eyesight when they are about seven years of age. Apart from that they appear well until they reach the age of eleven, when mental deterioration begins to set in. It is a slow process, so there is time for some kind of treatment. The late infantile type, however, is rapid. Everything happens almost at once between the ages of two and four – brain deterioration, blindness, the inability to walk. It happens so quickly there is no time for treatment.'

'Are you sure, are you really sure Charly has it?' asked Carmen, gripping Barry's hand. 'Couldn't it, couldn't it just be epilepsy after all?'

The doctor shook his head.

'Children with late infantile are often thought to have epilepsy when the condition first materialises,' he said.

'Sometimes they are just believed to be suffering some form of mental retardation. Adults are sometimes labelled schizophrenics. Often the first diagnostic clue comes with a visit to the opthalmologist who observes pathological changes in the retina. Additional tests of neurological and retinal function may help confirm suspicions. Skin biopsies when examined under an electron microscope have proved to be especially useful in establishing that it is Batten's disease and that is what we had to do with Charly.

'I'm afraid she has only three to four years to live and sadly during that time she will lose all her motor skills, go blind and have to be fed by tube.'

Carmen broke down. Barry put his arm around her, desperately trying to be strong.

'My little girl, my little baby. I won't see her grow up. Why is this happening to me?' she sobbed. 'Why is this happening to my Charly?'

Their world had just collapsed – and there was worse to come.

Barry sat holding his sobbing wife and staring at the doctor, who now said nothing. It was as if they were all suspended in a bubble of time, floating away from the real world of cars and traffic jams, mortgages and rents, children's tears and laughter.

Then it came to Barry in a flash. He didn't know why. He heard himself say the words, but it didn't sound like him.

'Will Rhys be affected, too?'

Carmen sat up, her tear-stained face pleading with the doctor.

'Possibly.'

Possibly. What did that mean? thought Barry.

Dr Wilson continued.

'We'll have to do some blood and skin tests on him, if you really wish to know at this stage.'

At thirteen months of age, Rhys had showed no physical signs of any disease. But they were told he now had a one in four chance of developing it. Barry and Carmen agreed to the tests.

There was no encouragement in the doctor's words. They just sat there staring vacantly. It was as if the doctor felt that Charly had an incurable disease and if they knew Rhys's fate it wouldn't make any difference.

They thanked him and it was all over.

They walked down the hospital corridor and out into the street. That was it. There was no operation that would put things right. No pills to make Charly better. It was the end of her life, a life that had not begun. And now a large bit of them had died too.

Charly and Rhys were being cared for in Walthamstow by Sue, the wife of one of Barry's cousins. Sue used to care for Charly when she was only four months old while Carmen went back to work to help make ends meet. Now they had to face her and tell her the news, tell Barry's mum and David too; tell the clan.

As they neared Sue's house, Barry spotted Uncle Brian and Auntie Pat. He pulled up and, oblivious to everything around him, including the traffic, ran across the road to them.

'Charly is going to die, Charly is going to die,' he said, breaking down in Brian's arms. 'She has only got three years to live.'

Carmen had got out of the car too and stood hugging Pat, all the emotion flooding out. The reality of the news was beginning to sink in. When would the tears stop flowing?

Rhys and Charly were both playing in the garden with Sue's three children, Kelly, Danny and Nikki. Barry and Carmen just stood and watched Charly running around playing so happily, so full of life. How could her life come to an end so suddenly?

They swept up their children in their arms and Carmen held on to Charly for a long time, longer than usual.

The news was unbearable for all the family. They couldn't believe what was happening when Barry told them over the telephone.

Barry and Carmen had to smile and be cheery and bustle about making tea and jam sandwiches and ironing pyjamas and feeding the rabbit and clearing up the toys and doing what normal, everyday families do during those first few hours back home. It was hard.

That evening Carmen went upstairs for a shower as Barry sat watching the television. But he wasn't really watching and he wasn't listening. He was just lost in a world of endless shapes flickering across the screen. He began to reflect on their lives, their beautiful children, how they both seemed so different.

The more he thought about it, the more a picture began to form in his mind. Charly had always been clumsy he realised. She had tripped up all the time, bumped into things. She had no fear, but things always went wrong. They knew somehow that she would stumble and fall down and they had always been there to catch her, or watch her. They hadn't thought anything of it then. She was healthy, happy, and life was good. These things happened to kids, didn't they? When Rhys began to walk, he was fearless too. Jumping on sofas, kicking balls in the park, romping with his father. But he never fell, stumbled, tripped or bumped into things.

Carmen tossed her head and shook out her wet hair. Then she inhaled deeply, pulling herself together, and her breath came out in a little shudder like Charly's and Rhys's did when they were heartbroken.

When she came downstairs Barry was waiting for her, leaning against the oven staring into the empty beer can he had squashed in his hand. He looked up, tears filling his eyes. She put her arms around him. He was her best friend, her dearest friend.

'I can't manage without you,' she said.

'You seem to be doing just fine,' he said, holding her now around the hips. He pulled her close and held her fast for a moment. He didn't kiss her, or argue with her or reason with her about their desperate situation. He was just grateful to have her friendship – and, he hoped, her love.

The next morning she woke at 7.30 a.m. when the alarm clock went off, to find that she was alone. She got up and looked around. Barry had left a note for her:

> *Sorry to leave without saying goodbye. Am going into the office to clear up a few things and telephone Great Ormond Street. Then I'm off to the doctors – and then the library. I want to find out what an enzyme really is! Love Barry.*

His battle had begun. From that morning on Barry was telephoning the world – Israel, America, Germany, Switzerland, South Africa, anywhere he had friends who could find out about Batten's disease, anywhere anyone could tell him there was hope.

Carmen was tired but wired up. Too many things had happened. Were happening. Was yesterday a dream? She looked in on Charly and Rhys who were still asleep, then went down the stairs. The curtains were still drawn and she walked through the darkened house and into the kitchen. She put the kettle on and stood over the cup staring down at the tea-bag. The kettle boiled and she just walked way. She didn't really want a drink at all.

A few days later on a chilly, cloudy and grey morning, Barry, Carmen, Charly and Rhys drove down to see David in Great Barton, Suffolk. The weather suited their mood. David was deeply upset when they broke the news to him. Barry and Carmen realised then that they had the whole support of the family. But they didn't really know what they needed. It all seemed a terrible nightmare that they would soon wake up from. Then everything would be all right.

The following month Barry and Carmen sat for what seemed like hours at the breakfast table. They buttered toast and opened pots of marmalade and jam. But they didn't eat. They sat drinking one coffee after another that neither of them wanted. They talked in fits and starts, as if conversation was some kind of rusty contraption that hadn't had much recent use. Now and then Barry made her smile. Now and then Carmen made him laugh. Now and then they drifted off into their own thoughts, a mixture of anxiety and hope. The world suddenly seemed a very odd place. Then, without speaking, they both automatically rose from the breakfast table and began to clear up. Barry washed and Carmen wiped. The telephone rang. They looked at each other. It was Friday, 13 March. Was this the call they had feared?

Barry sat at the bottom of the stairs clutching the receiver, the words of Dr Wilson's assistant, Celia Mostyn, echoing in his ears.

'I'm so sorry Mr Daniels, but Rhys's tests are positive.'

Carmen appeared in the doorway and knew by the look on her husband's face that this was it. The call she had prayed would never come. Her legs almost went from under her.

Barry tried to be strong, but it was hard. Trying to accept that one of his children had a terminal illness and wouldn't see her tenth birthday was tough enough. But for a mother and father to take on the news that both their children were going to die from a

92

disease they knew nothing about was impossible. The news was destroying all their lives.

Carmen was inconsolable. Barry cuddled her and said the right things. But as he held her close he wondered how he could keep up the pretence of being strong. He knew he had to — to save his family from falling apart.

When he told his mother the news, she seemed to handle it quite well. But he knew she was really hurting. Her only grandchildren were dying in front of her eyes. It was a terrible prospect for them all to face.

Barry stood back and admired the living room.

'There, what do you think?' he asked Carmen and his mother.

'It doesn't match up,' said Carmen. 'The wallpaper pattern doesn't follow through over there.' She pointed to the corner by the fireplace, where Barry's father had kept his books and knick-knacks.

'Your father did that once and hoped no one would notice. But I did. You know how meticulous he was when he decorated,' said his mother, gently mocking him.

'It's not obvious,' said Barry, defensively.

'It's very nice, Baz,' said Carmen, giving the shoulders of her hurt-looking, interior-designer husband a squeeze. He had only decorated the room to keep himself busy, to take his mind off everything else.

The next morning Barry was in the kitchen making a pot of tea when his mother called out to him.

'What is it, mum?' he answered and went into the living room.

'I told you your father was watching when you put up that wallpaper.'

Barry looked across at the corner by the fireplace and about a foot of the wallpaper was hanging down from the wall.

'Oh, sod it,' he said and stomped off into the kitchen with a wave of his hand.

The next day they all stood looking at the corner again, Barry, his mother and Carmen. The wallpaper was stuck back up.

'Who did that?' Barry asked. Both Carmen and his mother denied touching it. For the next few months, when things were really bad, when he and Carmen and his mother felt really depressed, in deep despair, they would find the wallpaper hanging down. When things seemed to get better it would mysteriously be stuck up again in the morning. Barry knew in his heart that it was something to do with the heat of the room – or was it?

Barry pushed the telephone against his ear and stared out of the kitchen window at the March wind and rain whipping against his father's greenhouse. On the other end of the line was Edie Dockter from the Batten's Disease Support and Research Association in New York. She was a spark of light at the end of a very dark tunnel. Edie had already lost one daughter to Batten's disease but now she was going down the same, long, heartbreaking road with her two disease-stricken sons, Tommy and Ken. Her words seemed to give Barry some sort of comfort. Edie promised to send him all the information she had on the illness and he promised to call her once he had read it.

Over the next few weeks Barry felt helpless. He was a carer, a nurse, a comforter and not a solver of problems. He wanted to get things done. Now he was living on the edge all right, but not the kind of edge he had been seeking all his life. He turned to his guitar, as he had done so many times before. Slowly, painstakingly, he wrote a song and called it 'Love's So Hard – Save The Children'.

'Barry, it's beautiful,' said Carmen.

'No, it's not. It's just my anthem of what we are going through,' he said.

The April showers pounded the car on the way to Gatwick airport, but Barry and Carmen didn't care. They were heading for the sunshine of Lanzarote. Life had to go on and they had to get away from dismal Britain, the memories and the despair.

Ahead of them were two weeks on an island in the Canaries, surrounded by white, Atlantic breakers and golden sand. Rhys and Charly were excited. Barry's cousin Pete, his wife Trish and their two children, Mica and Connor, were going with them.

It was a family holiday they would never forget. From the moment they stepped off the plane on to the blistering tarmac it was as if they had left all their troubles behind. Rhys loved the water and Charly lay on Barry's stomach as they floated in the shallow pool in the afternoon sun. It was a great break, time to reflect on the last couple of months. Now it all seemed so far away. Slowly, surely, Barry and Carmen began to plan a way forward.

Barry lay on the bed looking at the darkening blue sky that spun from the window across to the coast of Africa.

Unable to sleep, he had grown weary of the hard Spanish mattress. He eased himself up, careful not to wake Carmen, and walked out on to the balcony.

He stared at the night sky, the intricate yet ordered patterns of the stars burning in the deep vault of the heavens: Orion's Belt, the Great Bear, the solitary shining jewel of the North Star. He felt somehow he was waiting to die. But he wasn't frightened. He looked back into the room at Carmen, sleeping in the deep sleep of too much sangria, then he looked up again at the Great Bear.

'Dad, if you are there, please help me,' he said quietly.

5: Germany Calling

Barry stood at the end of the garden and looked across at the greenhouse his father had always pottered around in.

'For Christ's sake!' he shouted, not caring who heard him.

Christ? Who was he really?

He remembered his father's death and how he had sat in St John's Church trying to understand why he had lost a man who had worked hard all his life and never hurt anyone. Why had such a kind, caring man been taken away before his time?

Now, in his mind, Barry was questioning the existence of God.

'We thanked you for two, perfectly formed, healthy, beautiful children,' Barry said, looking at the sky where heaven was supposed to be. 'And now this is what you do to us!'

Barry knew now that he would find it difficult to believe anyone who told him that God was doing good in the world. Anyone who told him that God would heal all.

'Believe in him and he will save you. What kind of crap is that?' he asked out loud, clenching his fist at the

God he no longer believed was there.

A flock of starlings appeared as the sky suddenly turned from blue to grey, choosing the silver birch in his garden to tumble into like a pack of black playing cards sprinkled from the clouds.

Barry felt a hand on his shoulder and he turned around. It was Carmen.

'Who are you talking to, Baz?' she asked.

'Oh, him up there, if there is a him.'

She smiled. 'Come on in. Charly and Rhys want you. It's getting cold.'

'You know, Carmen, we had two perfect children, a beautiful, blonde, three-year-old girl, running, jumping, shouting, laughing, doing all the normal things that little children do. Then take away her legs, her ability to talk and laugh and see –'

He paused for a moment.

'Then throw in severe ataxia so that she cannot move her arms properly and is always uncomfortable. Then tell me Carmen that she will die in a year or two.'

He paused again. Carmen didn't speak. She knew what he meant, where he was coming from. She just let him go on.

'Then put me in front of this God and I'll ask him to explain why. Is this how God works?' Barry clenched his fist again and stared at it and Carmen put her arms around him.

'I know, I know. I feel the same too,' she said.

'He giveth and he taketh away,' said Barry sighing, as if accepting there was nothing he could do. 'Too many children die in this world – most of them in wars caused by religious arguments, by some stupid need for supremacy. But that's not what the ways of the Lord are about – or so we are told. What a bloody mess!'

The starlings fluttered about the tree looking like bats in the first dark shadows of moonlight.

'You know what I believe, Carmen?'

'What?'

'I believe God saw how corrupt us Earth people were becoming and packed his bags and moved to another slot in the solar system where he could start from scratch. He probably looked back and said: "Let them get on with it. They'll destroy themselves in the end!" '

By now Barry and Carmen were becoming more knowledgeable about Batten's disease and the Charly and Rhys Appeal they had set up was going well, with the help of friends, neighbours and local businessmen.

The aim was to raise enough money for a soft room to be built at their home where Rhys could romp in safety. It was too late for Charly now. She spent most of her day lying down. But Barry was motoring. He hired a studio in London with his friend Steve Braithwaite and singer Rose Patterson, known as Lateez, and recorded his new song 'Love's So Hard' for a cassette pack to raise the money so desperately needed for the appeal fund. He had to do something; he couldn't just sit and watch his children deteriorate. Another friend, Kate Carr, was a great help with the project. She designed and compiled a five-page colour booklet for the cassette, which carried all the information and things Barry wanted to say about the battle against Batten's disease. A beautiful photograph of Charly and Rhys was used for the front cover and Barry and Carmen were very moved with the end result.

Then came the break Barry had been praying for.

Edie rang from the Batten's Disease Registry located at the Institute for Basic Research in Staten Island, New York. She sounded excited. There was an international conference on the disease in Hamburg in a few weeks' time. Barry was determined to go. He wanted to know more than he was being told by doctors in Britain. He and Carmen had already been to see a genetic counselling specialist, Dr Baritser, at Great Ormond Street where they had been told there was no carrier testing. The defective genes inherited by them may have been in their families for hundreds of years or could just have been a chromosome mismatch at conception. There was no way of telling for sure.

A few weeks later they were on their way to Hamburg in a Saab borrowed from Barry's brother David. It was a long, tiring trip down to Dover and over to Calais on the ferry. From there it was a seven-hour drive through Belgium, Holland and into Germany where they headed down towards the Elbe River and Hamburg, a city that had risen like a phoenix from the ashes of the Second World War. Carmen studied the map as Barry drove through the streets that led to the port, one of the largest and busiest in Europe where cargoes of oil, iron ore, copper, wheat and cotton were being unloaded for the local industries. Barry was tired but he didn't mind; he was doing something positive for Charly and Rhys. Perhaps something good would come out of it all. Perhaps another door would open. Somehow he took a wrong turning again and they found themselves driving by the Aussenalster, the largest lake to be found in the centre of any city in Europe. Barry loved the feel of the place, the sailing boats and windsurfers, the grassy banks busy with joggers and strollers. He had a good feeling about Hamburg, a feeling of optimism.

When they finally arrived at their hotel in the small town of Wedel about half an hour from the conference centre, Barry and Carmen were pleased to find other parents whose children were victims of the disease – including Edie from America. It was an emotional meeting. Edie with all her suffering was proving to be such a strength for them. At last they didn't feel alone. Sharing their heartbreak with others, especially Edie, was a sort of release. Together, they all planned their conference visits, discussing which lectures to attend and what doctors to try and see.

Barry flicked through the agenda. The conference had been organised by Professor Kolschutter who was researching and treating patients with Batten's disease in Germany. One lecture particularly caught Barry's eye. On Friday, 12 June at 11.20 a.m., R. D. Jolly was talking about the usefulness of animal models in combating Batten's disease. He would discuss bone marrow transplants already being carried out on dogs.

The next day Barry and Carmen were at the conference bright and early. They didn't want to miss anything. But by lunchtime their heads were spinning. They felt out of their depth. It had been difficult to understand the presentations of the scientists. Barry had just sat scribbling madly, hoping it would all make sense at some point. He and Carmen mingled at every coffee break and meal stop, asking the simplest of questions. Soon everyone knew who they were.

The German doctor cleared his throat and began.

'Bone marrow transplantation has been successfully used to treat a wide variety of genetic diseases, including lysosomal storage disorders,' he told the packed lecture room.

'Lyso what?' Carmen asked Barry. Before he could answer, the American woman sitting next to her leant forward and whispered in her ear.

'Lysosomes, honey. They're what you could call factories busy producing things in our white cells.'

'Thanks,' said Carmen. She thought she understood. Barry smiled and kept scribbling his notes.

'As we know, enzymes are manufactured somewhere in our white cells and transported to the lysosome elsewhere in these cells,' said the doctor, adjusting his spectacles and pausing for a moment to read his notes.

'White cells are produced by our bone marrow. The rationale for the use of bone marrow transplantation in a lysosomal storage disorder, therefore, is that the enzyme that is lacking is a product of a cell that is itself produced by the bone marrow. Replacing the defective cell permanently can therefore be achieved by performing a bone marrow transplant.'

As the days went on, Barry heard more and more about bone marrow transplants but this time on animals. Disorders bearing a striking resemblance to Batten's disease had been diagnosed in dogs and sheep. The disease process had been closely monitored by scientists and there had been lengthy studies of the biochemical features and treatments. Finally, it had been decided to investigate the possibilities of bone marrow transplants. Four affected dogs, identified as having the disease by brain biopsies, were transplanted at five months of age from identical litter mates following irradiation.

The dogs then developed normally, up until the age of sixteen months when clinical features of the disease began to appear. There was loss of co-ordination, a staggering gait and impaired vision in all four animals.

Above: July 1986. A romantic visit to Venice during Barry and Carmen's first holiday together.

Right: 26 September 1987. Barry and Carmen's wedding at Epping registry office.

Above: Two-year-old Charly plays the big sister to Rhys, only two weeks old.

Left: Rhys sits pretty for the camera at eight months.

Above: Charly at
eighteen months –
a beautiful little star.

Right: June 1990.
Two-year-old
Charly poses with
her doll.

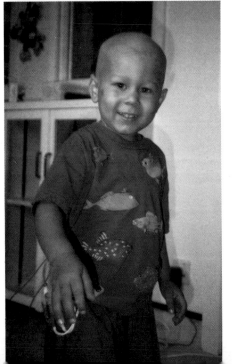

Above: Barry, Carmen, Rhys and Charly in May 1992, following Great Ormond Street's confirmation of Batten's disease in Charly and Rhys.

Left: Rhys, bright as a button in isolation following the first bone marrow transplant.

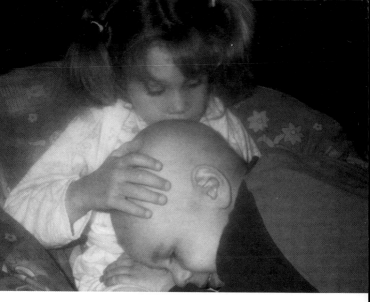

Above: Hugs and kisses for Rhys when he comes home from Bristol after the first transplant.

Below: Charly shares a smile with Dad in High Beach, Epping Forest.

Left: Rhys makes friends with a horse in Epping Forest the day before he leaves home for his second bone marrow transplant.

Right: Charly and Rhys with Fred Flintstone in Universal Studios, Florida, in March 1993.

Below: Charly snuggles down in her lovely new beanbag.

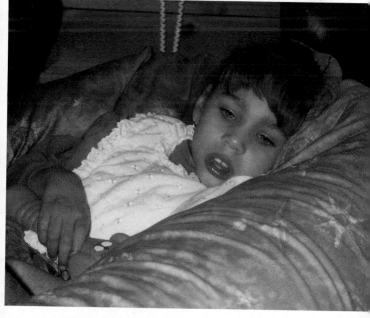

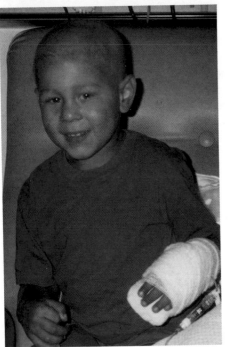

Above: 17 June 1993. Rhys salutes the hordes of waiting cameramen (*Guardian*).

Left: Rhys fights his way back to health after his second transplant in September 1994.

Two of them died a spontaneous death and the other two were put down eighteen months after the transplant because of severe disease progression.

Autopsies were performed and examination of the dogs' brains revealed a thickening of the dura mater, the outermost membrane covering. There were also signs of cerebral atrophy – a loss of brain tissue.

The conclusion was reached that ceroid lipofuscinosis could not be treated by bone marrow transplantation. But the overall failure of the experiment in the dogs did not necessarily mean that the transplant would not work on humans, the doctors believed. For it was not clear that the disease in animals was identical to the human disease. Even if it was identical, it did not mean it was identical to the late infantile variety, they argued. And it was difficult to know whether asymptomatic disease in dogs represented the same early stage as asymptomatic disease in humans. An asymptomatic child could be at an earlier stage of the disease and therefore stand a better chance of responding to the bone marrow treatment. All in all, it was difficult to evaluate the possibilities for humans from the results of transplants on dogs.

The next day, at the first opportunity, Barry grabbed Professor Brian Lake who was taking part in the conference. Professor Lake had diagnosed both Charly and Rhys at Great Ormond Street.

'What about the possibility of a bone marrow transplant on Rhys, now that he is pre-symptomatic?' Barry blurted out, half expecting the professor to shake his head. He didn't.

'It could be worth a try, if we can get someone interested in taking it on,' he said.

Barry felt a swell of hope rise in his heart. The

condition had never been treated this way before anywhere in the world so Rhys would be the first. Such an experiment could present complications. But if there was just the slightest chance, the word 'maybe' was all Barry needed to hear.

Next came Professor Mark Gardiner. His team was working on locating the markers for the defective genes causing Batten's disease. He told Barry to telephone Professor John Hobbs at the Westminster Children's Hospital. If anyone could do it, it would be him. Barry almost shook with emotion.

The last day of the conference was parents' question time. Barry had his questions all mapped out, but he expected a lack of enthusiasm for his plan after sitting through two hours of arguments during the lecture. He was right. As soon as he proposed that Rhys should undergo a bone marrow transplant the roof went up. Professor Lake and Dr Gardiner supported him, along with a few others. But 80 per cent of the packed lecture room were against it. Barry could not be deterred. There was no turning back. The 20 per cent of the audience supporting him was all he needed to start the battle.

The bone marrow transplants on dogs offered hope, but they were not totally successful – would they work on humans? By the end of the conference Barry could talk about nothing else as he and Carmen dined out with the families of other victims. His only other interest was the recipe for Hamburg's famous eel soup which he had come to love. Alongside the medical notes he had so painstakingly taken, he wrote: 'ham bone, smoked meat, carrots, celery, leeks, peas, dried fruit, vinegar, white wine, sugar, salt and eel. Yummy.' Carmen was not impressed.

Barry couldn't wait to get back home, much as he

had come to love the city with its restaurants, inns and harbour bars around the old fish market in the shadow of the magnificent castle. He couldn't wait to ring Professor Hobbs. On their last night they laughed with their new friends about the coach tour they had all taken late one afternoon which took them through the Reperbahn, Hamburg's notorious red light district. It had seemed just like lunchtime in Oxford Street, with people hurrying about and drinking coffee and disappearing into doorways and shopping. The only difference was that the window displays for silk undies weren't modelled by dummies. The women who sat putting their wares on show were all shapes and sizes.

'Oh well, I suppose there is something for everyone,' joked Carmen.

They toasted farewell to their friends with the traditional Hamburg drink *Lutt und Lutt*, a combination of a glass of lager chased by a small glass of corn brandy, and the next morning Barry did the seven-hour drive to Calais in six.

But things never turn out the way people quite expect them to and back in Epping Barry came to a full stop. Professor Hobbs was away and wouldn't be back until early the following month. It wasn't any good moping around and so Barry and Carmen threw themselves into fund-raising for the Charly and Rhys Appeal, with lots of help from local people.

It was launched at the La Taverna club in the town and turned out to be a marvellous family affair. All the clan were there. That same day the Cock and Magpie pub in Epping Green, owned by soccer manager Terry Venables, also launched a fund-raising event. It was a scorching hot day and the 'bikers' pub car park was packed with BMW and Suzuki motorbikes and of course the aristocrats of them all, Harley Davidsons.

The gardens were full of craft stalls, including a tattooist. Barry nearly took the plunge but lost his nerve at the last minute. His favourite bit of the action was the live bands in the pub hall. That day the two events raised nearly £6,000. It was a great start.

By now things were growing more tense at home. There had been lots of arguments between Barry and his mother. She was always trying to help out, but Barry kept blowing a fuse, telling her that they were his kids, he knew best. Carmen kept stepping in to keep the peace. His mother was only doing what mothers do, he knew that. But it just wasn't working, what with all the stress and difficulty of caring for Charly and all the worry about Rhys. Charly was having difficult nights, tossing and turning and crying, keeping her grandmother awake.

One morning they sat down together, just the three of them, Barry, his mother and Carmen. There were some new flats just down the road which had been built by the baking trade and his mother thought they were wonderful. She had worked in the trade for many years and could qualify for one of them. They all agreed it would be for the best – and anyway, the converted farmhouse was only a five-minute walk away. Soon she had a new home, and she later told them that she hadn't felt so happy and settled for years.

Barry was in tears. He put the telephone down in his office at work, Professor Hobbs's words still ringing in his ears.

'As soon as we get all your tissue types we can start the search for a donor.'

The professor already knew about Rhys's case and was prepared to go ahead with the revolutionary transplant. Barry was so choked up he could hardly speak.

'You don't know what this means to us, professor. Thank you. Thank you from all of us.'

It was a baking hot morning the next day when Barry, Carmen, Rhys and Charly arrived at St Margaret's Hospital to have blood tests. The sort of bright morning that made the world seem a better place, that made people moan about sitting in offices and factories, that brought the promise of early evening strolls by the river and deckchairs in the garden.

The samples were to be sent to the Blood Transfusion Service at Brentwood Hospital in Essex for tissue typing and then quickly on to Professor Hobbs and his team at the Westminster. They spent almost the whole morning in the cramped hospital corridor while forms were filled in and questions asked. But it didn't matter; it was worth it. Another day, another hospital, another battle. The race was on to save Rhys from the onset of Batten's disease and that was all Barry and Carmen cared about.

But the fight was still going on to help little Charly, who by now had started to lose the use of her legs and her ability to communicate. Days later, Barry and Carmen flew to Milan to see Dr Claudio Bordignon, a leading specialist in the research into gene therapy.

Genetic and part-genetic diseases affect one in every twenty people in the world by the age of 25 and as many as two in three people in the course of a natural lifetime. Of more than 4,000 known inherited disorders, most lack fully effective therapies.

At that time the positions of only four per cent of the estimated 100,000 human genes had been located, but scientists around the world were engaged in an ambitious human gene project to map the rest. Such a

107

project would take years, perhaps tens of years and cost billions of pounds, but it was obvious that it offered the chance to prevent or cure terrible scourges such as cystic fibrosis, muscular dystrophy, haemophilia and Batten's disease. Treatment of some forms of heart disease, as well as cancer and AIDS, was also a possibility.

Barry had been told that strict controls on such work were essential and would perhaps hold up the miracle process. He understood that. There could, after all, be abuses. There was the prospect of a brave new world in which the state predetermined the IQ of all newborn babies.

It was the discovery in 1953 of the DNA double helix – the genetic blueprint of life – by American biologist Jim Watson and British physicist Francis Crick that opened the door to gene therapy and other major advances that would one day dramatically improve life. Now Barry was pinning his hopes on them.

In his little office at the San Raphael Hospital, Dr Bordignon explained that gene therapy was a possibility for Charly, but first the defective gene that caused the disease had to be located and that was down to Professor Mark Gardiner and his team at University College Hospital. Finding that needle in a haystack was a gigantic task. Only when it was successfully completed could therapy be directed towards increasing the body's metabolism or blocking the formation of the toxic product that caused the disease by diet or drug therapy. If the rogue gene directed the production of a defective enzyme or hormone, therapy could be directed towards enzyme or hormone replacement. Other choices, it seemed, would involve the transplant of glial cells from an individual with a normal gene and reintroducing them into the brain of the victim. But there was another theory too. Since it was believed that some types of Batten's disease had an adult or delayed onset, doctors might be able to programme it to very late in life – say at the age of 80. Barry left feeling he had built up useful contacts. The medical world and victims' families in Europe and America were beginning to hear about him. In some way he was becoming a catalyst of hope in the search to find a cure, a contact point, a sort of beacon in the darkness of the much-feared unknown.

Barry picked up the post from the doormat and hurriedly opened the big airmail envelope from America.

'We'll read this tonight,' he told Carmen, putting the pile of fact sheets on the table. He gulped down a mug of tea and rushed out of the door to work.

That evening, when Charly and Rhys were sleeping, they sat on the floor by the fireside. Barry had one hand on Carmen's shoulder and the other held the new information on Batten's disease sent to them by an American magazine.

'Apparently, it's more common in Finland and Sweden,' said Barry. Carmen looked down at the fact sheet in his hand, but she wasn't really reading it. She just wanted to listen. Funny, but she couldn't remember if Charly had drunk her milky cocoa before she fell asleep or not.

Barry read on: 'It is also quite common in other parts of Northern Europe as well as Newfoundland and Canada. The first instances of the condition were probably reported by a bloke called Dr Stengel in 1826 who described four affected children, all related, in a small mining community in Norway. Listen to this:

'Batten's disease often strikes multiple children in the same family because of the inherited defective gene. It is estimated to affect up to one in every 12,500 births, according to the *American Journal of Medical Genetics*. Batten's disease is the most common neuro-genetic storage disorder occurring in children.'

Strange, but suddenly Carmen took comfort in the fact that they were not really alone, just as she did when they were in Hamburg. There were hundreds of other parents feeling as wrecked as they did. Thousands even. Millions? No, not millions, she was just being silly. 'Go on,' she said.

'You won't like this. I don't.' Barry paused for a moment. 'No treatment is known to halt or reverse the effects of Batten's disease, but vitamin therapy has reportedly stabilised some patients for a short time. Seizures can be controlled with drugs, but most treat-ment focuses on support for the families, helping them cope with the profound disabilities and dementia of the disease as well as the years of emotional trauma and medical bills.'

He looked down at Carmen: she was asleep, exhausted. Barry didn't speak any more, but con-tinued to read on silently to himself.

He was fascinated by the story of a young American boy who had developed the disease in the early 1970s. There was no history of his parents being related by any kind of blood ties.

The patient was the second child and first-born son of his parents. They had a daughter, two years older, who was well. The boy was born after a full-term pregnancy that was complicated by pre-eclampsia, a serious condition which if not treated can lead to a toxic state and high blood pressure for the mother.

After being delivered by forceps the boy suffered apnoea, a temporary inability to breathe, and a tube had to be inserted into his windpipe.

Although, as the months went on, he passed his early development milestones at a later age than his sister, he was considered normal by his mother and family doctor until he got to three years of age.

At this time he began to develop seizures which had to be controlled by drugs such as phenobarbitone and diazepam.

Then came a rapid deterioration of his intellectual and motor functions, followed by longer seizures. Within five months the boy could no longer walk; by seven months, after the onset of the symptoms, he was mute and after ten months he no longer appeared to recognise his mother. He was admitted to the Bronx Municipal Hospital in New York at the age of four years and two months, one year after his first seizure. Vital signs, height and weight, seemed normal. Results of a general physical examination were normal too. There were no apparent body abnormalities. When medications were reduced, however, he became generally alert, smiled socially and followed the doctors visually. He talked but did not show any receptive language function. In other words, he didn't really answer. His personal social development was below the American medical standard.

When doctors examined his eyes, they found pigmentary degeneration of the macula, the coloured area. But there was no definite pallor of the optic discs and the doctors were baffled. There was no limitation of gaze either.

By now the little boy was unable to sit without support. When he was awake there were frequent tremulous and jerky movements of the hands, feet and tongue.

When he was pricked with a pin, there was an appropriate, affective response. Reflexes were brisk and his blood cell count, glucose levels, urinalyses and protein data were normal. The doctors were mystified.

Barry couldn't help thinking about the little boy. It was almost as if he wasn't a person at all but rather some kind of animal for experiment. The medical paper was so matter-of-fact, as matter-of-fact as the doctors who had diagnosed Charly and Rhys. He made himself read on. He had to know as much as he could about the disease.

The little boy continued having seizures while taking a variety of anti-convulsants. Just like Charly, Barry thought to himself. The patient was transferred to a residential treatment centre where he developed epilepsy and died fifteen months after the onset of his illness.

As much as Barry wanted to, he couldn't read on. It was all about the autopsy and biopsies, about the spinal cord being embedded in paraffin for examination, about the cerebrum, the ventricular system, the rubbery consistency of the brain, neurons and . . .

Barry dropped the sheets on the floor, his eyes growing heavy. As he put his head on Carmen's shoulder, he began to think of Charly's symptoms. They were much the same. Why hadn't the doctors been able to diagnose Batten's disease at the beginning? It seemed so obvious to him now, knowing what he knew. Still, did it matter whether they had done or not? He fell asleep leaning on his wife.

It was 3 a.m. when he woke up with cramp in his neck and managed to get Carmen to her feet. They staggered up to bed together and he wondered what the new day would bring. Inside he was frustrated. Red tape was holding things up. Professor Hobbs had already explained that because Rhys was the first child in the world to be put forward for a bone marrow transplant to combat Batten's disease, he would have to seek permission from the Medical Board of Ethics, a sometimes lengthy process. Barry knew that he couldn't buck the system. The Ethics Board was there for a good reason and he accepted that he would just have to be patient.

Barry picked up the envelope from the doormat and walked back into the kitchen.

'It's from the Westminster,' he said.

'Good news or bad?' asked Carmen, buttering some toast and pulling Rhys's fingers out of the marmalade jar.

'Neither. It's the consent form for the transplant.'

'Read it to me, then.' Carmen sat down wiping Rhys's sticky fingers.

Barry sighed and read the letter. It all seemed so matter-of-fact, so impersonal, like a hire purchase contract with lots of small print.

' "Your son Rhys Daniels is being considered for a bone marrow transplant," ' he read. ' "So far as is known, this has not previously been attempted in humans. Before a final decision can be made, there-fore, you should give fully informed consent." '

'That's understandable,' said Carmen. 'They've got to cover themselves in case anything goes wrong.'

Barry read on, not answering her. ' "It is, of course, essential that you understand not only the experimen-tal nature of the transplant but the risks involved *per se*." '

'Eat your toast: eat it, Rhys!' Carmen held the crispy slice to his mouth, but it was no good, he wasn't hungry.

'Go on,' she said. Barry flicked through the perfectly typed pages.

' "So far, we have been unable to find a perfectly matched donor for Rhys, related or unrelated. Four potential, volunteer, unrelated donors who have the same tissue type have been tested against him. All four have been found to react to him, and he to them. The risks of rejection and graft-versus-host disease are therefore considerably higher. However, it is difficult to say precisely what this risk might be in real terms. One would have to say, though, that his chances of survival would be less than 50 per cent, perhaps considerably less." '

Carmen put down the toast and picked up her son. Then she carried him out to the garden and they stood talking to their lop-eared rabbit, Bamu, in his hutch. Barry sat at the table staring at the pot of marmalade.

Business was booming for Barry's company and over the following few months he flew to Russia, Romania, Belgium, Israel, South Korea, Taiwan and even the Pacific island of Guam. Wherever he went he visited hospitals, universities and laboratories, seeking information on Batten's disease. In Moscow Barry was warmly welcomed at the Neurological Institute where he swapped notes through translators with other victims' families.

Back home the medical machine rolled on as the search for a perfect donor spread across Europe and America. Rhys was given more tests and Carmen was sick of seeing her son injected with one needle after another. But she told herself it would be worth it in the end. It just had to be.

More than ever Barry and Carmen were in desperate need of a soft room, a padded, cushioned area in their small house for the children, where they could be safe, where if Rhys tripped and fell he would not hurt himself and where Charly could lie comfortably.

Barry had plans drawn up for a small extension off the kitchen and sent them to the council for approval. But there was no way he could afford it. Luckily, his friends, headed by Jackie and Keith Davis and the rest of the local community, came to the rescue. The fund-raising for the Charly and Rhys Appeal was stepped up. The fire service joined in with the lads from the night watch pulling a fire engine through Epping High Street. There were fêtes and raffles, office collections and darts competitions, manor house garden parties and a donation box at the police station.

Finally, they raised enough money and when the council gave its approval Barry started to dig the first trench for the foundations. Friends joined in and hour by hour, brick by brick, the room grew. Old schoolfriend Terry Johnson, who now had a building company, took on the main brunt of the work and soon the extension was full of green and blue cushions and padded walls and hundreds of soft red and yellow balls. Friends and neighbours clapped and cheered as Rhys jumped and fell and tumbled about. This had to be party week.

The hot saucepan of chilli sizzled on the hob. Carmen hurried around filling bowls with crisps and peanuts and cleaning ashtrays. Barry had set up a bar on the kitchen table and stocked the fridge with cans of lager. The guests helped themselves to drinks, milling around the saucepan of chilli and baking tray full of hot garlic bread. About twenty people had gathered in the living room, although more were coming in the course of the evening. The men wore jeans, old faded jeans, and T-shirts or shirts with frayed collars. The women wore little or no make-up. They were all friends, there were no pretences. Barry had set out black, plastic rubbish sacks, which were steadily growing more bulky with empty beer cans. In one corner of the lounge six or seven people sat on the floor discussing politics. Barry avoided the conversation and turned up David Bowie's 'China Girl' on the stereo. He loved the action and he was going with the flow. Carmen was busy bringing plates of food to people. She felt as if she was among close friends. They had all helped in some way in the building of the soft room. This was her world. The veil of worry over Charly that had been suffocating her had gone away for a while like the fading memories of a nightmare. As the evening wore on Barry and Carmen watched and listened, talked and laughed. For a moment life seemed good.

Everyone was getting away from being bourgeois, avoiding entrapment in a life of boring money grabbing. Everyone was escaping mortality and ageing. They were all in Never Never Land, just like Peter Pan. The more drink they had, the bigger the dream and the louder the conversation. If only they weren't tainted by making money, if only they weren't enslaved by mortgages or rents; if only they weren't dependent on their jobs, they would stay forever young, carefree and happy.

When all the chilli had been eaten and people were just drinking, Carmen grew very tired. She couldn't be bothered to pick up the half-full beer cans scattered around the floor and on the tables and chairs and shelves. She couldn't be bothered to empty and clean the ashtrays any more. She just wanted everyone to go, as much as she enjoyed their friendship and the help they had given her family. She just wanted to be alone with Barry. To make music with him, her kind of music. To pray in their own kind of way that Charly wouldn't suffer any more pain.

How many more telephone calls like this could he take? How much more bad news in his life? Barry sat on the stairs with the telephone in his hand as he had done so many times before.

'Are you there, Barry?'

Ashok Vellodi was still on the line.

'Yes, I'm here.' There was no emotion in Barry's voice.

'We'll try elsewhere. Someone, somewhere, will do it,' said Ashok. 'Give me a call in the morning after you've talked to Carmen.'

Barry stood for a moment looking at Charly wrapped in a blanket on the sofa. He gave her a kiss on the cheek and went into the kitchen where Carmen was washing up.

'Who was that on the telephone?' she asked. Barry threw a ball to Rhys clambering around the soft room.

'It was Ashok. We've got ethical approval for the transplant.'

Carmen was overjoyed and went to say something, but stopped short, catching the look in her husband's eye.

'We've got the bloody approval and they can't bloody well do it!'

117

'Why not?'

'Because this useless Government is closing the place down!'

It was Monday, 23 November, another big day, another milestone on the way to a cure for Rhys. The Westminster Children's Hospital was closing the following March and the transplant had been called off. The bone marrow unit would be relocating to the new Chelsea and Westminster Hospital. But there was no guarantee of a transplant for Barry and Carmen's son. The nursing staff and other medical back-up personnel were being run down at the Westminster and it was no longer safe to attempt such a long, intricate process.

Barry and Carmen were shattered. All they had fought for, the very meaning of life itself, had been taken away at the stroke of Health Minister Virginia Bottomley's pen. It was the first time they had heard about the closure. No one had even warned them it was likely. How many more obstacles must they face?

But everyone kept going. The medical machine, driven by Professor Hobbs, chugged on, stubbornly, painstakingly. Barry and Carmen regarded him as their friend. The world looked on as they hunted for a donor. There were more tests at the Westminster for Rhys, hugs and kisses and words of comfort and encouragement for Barry and Carmen from the nursing staff.

'Thank you, thank you,' they said, passing from one nurse to another, one hospital orderly to another, one porter to another. None of them, including the consultants, knew what the future held for them. Barry nicknamed Westminster the Hospital of Despair.

* * *

Carmen woke to the sound of the wind on the window. For one blissful moment she thought she was back in the country, in the rambling old Essex house she grew up in. She could almost smell the hay and freshly cut grass of Alan and Sarah's farm. Charly and Rhys would have loved it.

It took Carmen several minutes to adjust to the present and the hotel bedroom. She turned and looked at Barry sleeping the deep sleep of tired men. The Paris traffic stirred her out of her thoughts. Why was it that she never remembered dreams very clearly afterwards? She had slept in fits and starts but she had dreamed something about Rhys and Charly and Mickey Mouse. Whatever she dreamed in the night had evoked a longing to go back in time. She got up without waking Barry and Rhys and Charly and sat at the small table in the room working out their finances to the last penny. It didn't look good. But all she and Barry needed was a chance to put everything right. Rhys and Charly had been given the key to Euro Disney thanks to the generosity of the Starlight Foundation. For four days it had rained, or was cloudy or windy, but Mickey, Goofy, Donald Duck, Snow White and the Disney management had laid out the red carpet for them. Charly couldn't take it all in. She couldn't walk now and could barely see. But for Rhys it was a fairytale come true and now he had a new friend he kept asking for – Pinocchio.

Things were moving fast. Ashok had checked with other possible bone marrow units, but Manchester Hospital and Great Ormond Street would only take Rhys on with a perfect-match donor, and even then they would not commit themselves. The Westminster could do the transplant now if only it had the facility.

For it was willing to use the mismatch donors and take that extra risk. Barry and Carmen felt cheated by the Health Service. Rhys was missing what could be his only chance of survival. They and everyone around them believed it was unfair.

Then came a message that raised Barry and Carmen's hopes. On Wednesday, 16 December, Barry's brother David had a telephone call from the American company he worked for, Sargent Incorporated, from its offices in New Haven, Connecticut. The company was willing to put up $250,000 for the transplant if it was done in the United States. It was a wonderful offer. Barry got in touch with bone marrow specialist Dr Krivitt at the Mayo Clinic in Minnesota. Sadly, their enthusiasm and hopes were snuffed out again like the flame of a candle.

Dr Krivitt was not convinced about the bone marrow transplant on Rhys. He felt that the best team in the world for such experimental treatment was Professor Hobbs and Dr Ashok Vellodi at the Westminster. It was a catch-22 situation.

On 22 December a lorry pulled up outside Barry's terraced house in Epping. It was children's store chief Sophie Mirman and her husband Richard's Christmas present for Charly and Rhys — tons of soft wood peelings for a safe play area in the garden and special toys. Uncle Charlie, Uncle Brian, Barry and his cousin Paul barrowed the peelings around the back of the house and half the garden began to disappear under a blanket of bark.

Christmas Day was painful. There were just the four of them. Charly didn't understand what was going on and Rhys was too young to take it all in. There were lots of quiet times, times spent reflecting on what might have been. Lots of tears on a day the rest of the street were celebrating.

Three days later, on 28 December, Rhys was two. The family party did little to cheer Barry and Carmen. The whole of Britain seemed to be sleeping, drinking and eating its way into the New Year. Barry needed everyone to be at their posts, be ready to help. He hadn't time to be festive. The clock wasn't on his side. He couldn't wait for the celebrations to end. On New Year's Eve he was on the telephone finding out about the blood tests on more members of his family. No luck, all were unmatched. On New Year's Day he rang Dr Krivitt in Minnesota again. One last go. But no, he would not transplant and certainly not without a sibling donor. However, he would give all his support to Professor Hobbs and his team. Barry quietly put down the telephone. Where now? All he had left was Professor Hobbs.

One door after another was being closed on Barry and Carmen. They went back to Great Ormond Street to see Dr Wilson, but he was not supportive of their intentions to give Rhys a bone marrow transplant. He just did not think it would work. They refused to be put off. They had met with the same reception in Hamburg.

It was a cold, bleak February in every respect. The wind howled against the living-room window day after day. It rained day after day too, the sort of icy rain that cut into the cheekbones and froze the jaw. Charly lay staring at the window and Rhys would run over and give her a kiss every now and then. Barry watched the telephone, as if willing it to ring, trying to pass thought waves down some imaginary line to the best doctors in Britain. Carmen brushed Charly's hair time and again and whispered in her ear.

121

This is no good, thought Barry. They all needed some sunshine, some fun, something to live for. He wanted Charly and Rhys to be like other children. By the end of the week he had booked a date with Mickey Mouse in Disneyworld.

Things felt different in Orlando, Florida. Barry felt he was living on a giant movie set, but then he knew America was like that. There were hamburgers and Coke, Mickey Mouse and Donald Duck and space rides with Rhys. Carmen began to laugh out loud again and Barry floated around a pool with Charly. Julie had gone with them to help look after Charly and Rhys.

Another reason for their trip was to visit New York to stay with Edie in Staten Island where they went to the Batten's disease research laboratories at 1050 Forest Hill Road. Ultrastructure Director Dr Krystina Wisniewski was keen on doing tests on Rhys and they agreed, giving blood samples from all the family. Krystina just could not believe that Rhys was affected by the illness. He was just so different from any other child she had seen with the condition.

Edie and her husband Gene took them around New York on the ferry and Barry and Carmen were totally blown away by the immense size of the Big Apple, its towering buildings. The days sped by and all too soon they were on a plane home to face whatever lay in store for them.

Barry's eyes swelled with tears as he walked down the long, grey hospital corridor looking at the boxes and packing cases. Teddy bears' legs and arms were sticking out of crates, piles of toy cars were on the floor and posters were hanging off the walls of the once world-renowned transplant unit.

122

In a little office at the Westminster Hospital Ashok Vellodi told him there was no good news. The bone marrow unit had not been found a new base. The nurses and doctors were in disarray. There wasn't a single sound of laughter anywhere in the building.

The telephone rang as Barry arrived home. It was the *Evening Standard*'s medical reporter, Jo Revill. She had just been to the Westminster and experienced what Barry had. The nurses were in tears. The famous unit which had been opened by Peter Bottomley thirteen years ago and had performed some of the world's pioneering transplant operations was now being closed by his wife.

The *Evening Standard* ran the story on page one with a colour picture of Charly and Rhys, highlighting the family's plight. Health Secretary Virginia Bottomley was being blamed for the disastrous planning of the new hospital, with MPs criticising lax management and a series of errors of judgement that had led to the centre costing almost twice as much as planned and being completed 25 weeks late.

The next day Jo rang again.

'A lawyer wants to talk to you,' she said.

Barry was suspicious. 'Who is he?'

'His name is Alan Meyer. He's the legal adviser to the Westminster Hospital's Development Fund and he wants to see you about the closure of the unit.'

Once again Barry was clutching at straws. Was another door opening? He just had to find out.

Several days later Rhys was headline news again. Alan Meyer believed Barry and Carmen had grounds to sue Virginia Bottomley, the Secretary of Health, for lack of consultation over the closure of the transplant unit.

Alan Meyer was a senior partner in the London firm

of solicitors Halsey Lightly. He had been involved in the case of Olivia Graham, a girl whose life was shattered by a hospital blunder that left her handicapped. Her family won £550,000 damages over negligence.

The media madness began and Barry's feet hardly touched the ground. The family were on BBC News, Channel 4's *Big Breakfast* and Radio Essex. And now all the major national newspapers picked up the story.

6: A Media Star Is Born

Barry sat on the plane staring out of the window down at the English Channel. It was a bad time to be flying to Algeria, but his company needed the contract. Still, he had left Carmen with some good news. The new donor tests were looking good and Ashok had felt more confident. But no hospital had come forward and he had wondered if he would have to strip naked and chain himself to the Houses of Parliament to get himself heard. The Government seemed to wonder what all the fuss was about. Letters were going back and forth between him and Virginia Bottomley. She claimed there were at least eight other bone marrow transplant centres – but she just didn't seem to grasp the fact that none of them would agree to carry out the treatment on his son, whereas the Westminster had been willing to do so.

Barry and Carmen had been invited to see Dr Tony Oakhill at Bristol's Children's Hospital. It had been a positive meeting. But again they were entangled in red tape. Nothing could be done until the Bristol Ethical Review Committee had seen the report on Rhys and Dr Oakhill had assessed the available donors. It was still a waiting game.

Barry's thoughts were interrupted by the air hostess offering breakfast. He declined and just took the coffee. Eating was not something he did much of these days.

The plane swept into Algiers airport and the doors opened to a hail of gunfire somewhere in the city.

'What the hell is that?' he asked the stewardess.

'That's Algeria,' she answered, hurrying the passengers out on to the tarmac. They sped off to the terminal building in the waiting coach, gunfire ringing in their ears.

Korean construction company officials tried to put Barry in a sort of communal shack, but he refused. He checked into a nearby hotel and didn't move outside until it was time to get the flight back. Not the best way to do business, he thought. Rhys needed him to be alive and kicking in England, not dead and buried in Algeria. 'I'm outa here!'

A week later he was back home – and hope was just around the corner. For on Monday, 26 April, Mr Justice Popplewell granted leave for Barry and Carmen to apply for a judicial review of their case in the High Court. Battles were beginning to be won.

The *Guardian* newspaper ran an exclusive story on the legal case and the granting of the review. The next day the world's media were camped on Barry's doorstep, along with ITN, the BBC and Sky TV. Rhys was a little megastar.

Carmen picked up the telephone and took a deep breath. It was yet another reporter and she wanted to say the right things. The things she meant in her heart. She prayed they would come out right and the girl on the other end of the line wouldn't misquote her.

'Yes, it fills me with disgust that my little boy can't

126

be treated. Yes, this treatment is expensive. That's right, the disease doesn't strike many children – but does that make it less important?'

She passed the telephone to Barry.

'Hello, it's Barry here.'

The reporter tap-danced with her questions, switching easily from one point to another. Barry listened quietly, looking over at Carmen brushing Charly's hair on the sofa.

'To look at Rhys now, you just see a boisterous happy two-year-old,' he said. 'But seeing Charly deteriorate, we know how soon that could happen to our son. Time is ticking away while the bureaucrats row about funding.

'There are breakthroughs being made in genetic therapy every day. Meanwhile we'll do whatever we can to save our children and others suffering from this terrible disease. We both know we've got to try anything that offers us even the slightest hope of success. We've got to put on a brave face and make our babies' lives as happy as we can. We're praying for a miracle, but what else can we do?'

The reporter later managed to get through to Ashok whose team was hoping to replenish Rhys's body with marrow-making, healthy white blood cells.

'True, the evidence to support the transplant is slender and a perfect donor has not yet been found,' he said. 'But it is the only chance the Daniels have of saving their son.'

Ashok was being moved to a general ward at the new Chelsea and Westminster Hospital, to carry out follow-up treatment on children but without the possibility of offering them transplants. He had been told his unit had been disbanded because of funding difficulties for the expensive treatment. The average bone marrow transplant cost £42,000 and they had been doing only ten such operations a year.

Barry had rung the regional health authority to complain.

'We have to point out to everyone that we can only commit the money to the unit if it can guarantee payment for twelve transplants or ideally twenty-five a year,' said the woman on the other end of the line.

Already local businesses were rallying round in a bid to raise money to buy special equipment for Barry and Carmen's home. And many companies in the area had pledged to pay for flights to America if treatment was made available. But Barry had another idea, one desperate plan.

'I don't care what it costs. Just sort it out!'

They all sat around the boardroom table looking down at Mohamed Al Fayed on his hands and knees. The Harrods boss was romping with Rhys and Charly on the floor under a life-size toy donkey. Every time the multi-millionaire store chief pressed a button its eyes lit up, it nodded its head, wagged its tail and neighed.

Harrods' public relations chief Michael Cole looked across at Dr Ashok Vellodi, Barry, Alan Meyer and health authority representative Sheila Adam and smiled.

'Well, ladies and gentlemen, shall we proceed?'

Following his success at getting the judicial review, Barry and Carmen with Rhys had appeared live on Sky TV with presenter Selina Scott to talk about Rhys and Charly, his fears and his hopes and the heartbreak they had suffered over the closure of Westminster Children's Hospital.

Mohamed Al Fayed had been watching the programme at home with his family.

The next evening Selina rang Barry for a live telephone link-up. She had an anonymous offer to help pay for the costs of Rhys's transplant – and the accommodation for Barry and Carmen while the long medical process was undertaken. The name of the benefactor didn't stay secret for long – Selina leaked Mr Al Fayed's name on air.

The next morning Harrods' PR supremo Michael Cole came on the telephone to Barry.

'We're sending a car for you!' he said. 'Mr Al Fayed wants to see you and Carmen and the children.'

Newspaper photographers, reporters and TV cameramen jostled each other outside the top Knightsbridge store as Barry, Carmen, Charly and Rhys arrived in a black limousine.

In the stately, wood-panelled boardroom Mohamed Al Fayed acted more like a father than a millionaire businessman. He was offering his financial and legal support, whatever was needed. Barry and Carmen were overwhelmed as he joked that Rhys was the only little boy ever to walk across his long, leather-topped executive table.

'Now bring in the donkey!' he ordered and the huge, baying, toy animal was wheeled in.

The following few days were hectic. There were neurophysiological tests on Rhys at Great Ormond Street, the BBC and Sky TV were waiting for Barry wherever he went, Malcolm Thomas of the British Bone Marrow Donor Appeal rang to say he was checking all panels for Rhys's tissue type and, finally, Barry and Carmen and Rhys checked into Bristol Children's Hospital for new transplant investigations.

Everyone was hoping against hope. Dr Tony Oakhill was on side. Barry and Carmen liked him and they had made another new friend, transplant co-ordinator Dr

Jackie Cornish. Three days later on the drive home Barry and Carmen were excited. They kept saying the same thing over and over again – it will work, won't it?

'I've got a really strong feeling that the faith I have in what we are doing will pull us through this, somehow,' said Barry.

Later that night at home they went through their post, sitting by the fire as they always did, drinking a bottle of wine to dull the pain. There were the normal bills that people get, gas, electricity, TV licence. They wondered how they would pay them, as decent people do. But it was the official-looking, white envelope with the neatly typed address they pondered over before opening. It was a letter from their lawyer. The court date for the fight against the closure of Westminster Children's Hospital by the Secretary of State, Virginia Bottomley, had been set for 9 June.

The media were out in force that morning when Barry, Carmen, Charly and Rhys arrived at the High Court in the Strand. Cameras clicked and microphones were thrust in their faces, but they didn't care. They needed all the exposure they could get. They had gone public now: it was the only way to fight the Establishment that wasn't on their side. They had to batter down more doors. There was no alternative: they had come this far, they couldn't just go backwards, or crumble, or hide.

Barry sat on a wooden bench in the courtroom as his QC told the judges that the decision by Health Secretary Virginia Bottomley to close the pioneering bone marrow transplant unit at the Westminster was like 'an act of God' which may have condemned two-year-old Rhys to death. He also branded the decision 'unlawful'.

Barry and Carmen were seeking a declaration that the unit should never have been closed. They also accused Virginia Bottomley and the two health authorities concerned, Riverside and North-West Thames, of failing to comply with proper consultation procedures.

The judges were told that Rhys suffered from Batten's disease, an inherited, metabolic disorder which caused blindness, dementia and death, usually by the age of seven. He had been offered treatment at Bristol's Royal Hospital for Sick Children and Harrods' chairman Mohamed Al Fayed had offered to pay for private treatment.

But Mr Patrick Milmo QC said approval had yet to be given by the Ethical Review Committee at Bristol and a donor still had to be found. He told Lord Justice Kennedy and Mr Justice Macpherson that, if nothing else, the result of the judicial review 'may act as a spur to those who have control over Rhys's further treatment'.

He added: 'Little Rhys was a victim of a sorry chain of events which saw the bone marrow unit at Westminster Children's Hospital disappear without human intervention and control much like an act of God – rather like a cliff crumbling into the sea.'

A bone marrow transplant was the only treatment which might cure Rhys, the judges heard.

With six months to go before his third birthday and treatment taking three months, 'we are perilously close to the deadline,' Mr Milmo said.

Barry stared hard at the judges. They seemed to be taking it all in; they looked sympathetic.

Mr Milmo told them that when Rhys was first diagnosed at Great Ormond Street Hospital, his parents were advised that there was no cure and no hope.

'But they showed energy, resourcefulness and determination,' he said, walking up and down. 'And last July Rhys was placed at the head of the list for the transplant at the Westminster.

'The unit was developing and practising one of the most advanced technical procedures in the medical world for the benefit of one of the most tragic categories of illness among children in the world.'

But the judges heard that eight months later, in April, the hospital was allowed to close with Rhys the only child promised treatment still waiting.

Mr Milmo said it had originally been planned that when the hospital closed the transplant unit would be transferred to the new Chelsea and Westminster Hospital. However, in the later stages of construction the previous year, there appeared to have been a change of plan. How that came about was not wholly clear, but it was at the time of fundamental changes in the funding and organisation of the National Health Service, the introduction of the NHS trusts and the concept of the internal market. There was evidence of misgivings that the unit would not be cost-effective or viable. The area planned for it at the Chelsea and Westminster Hospital was now used as a furniture store.

Mr Milmo said that in itself was sufficient comment on the lack of proper funding and competent planning and administration in the public health service in London. It revealed not only the deficiencies in planning and administration but also a lack of consultation and proper decision making in accordance with the requirements of the law.

'We say the decisions which were made or should have been made required consultation with at least the local community health council before they were finalised or put into effect,' he added. Barry almost clapped.

When the court adjourned, Barry walked out into the sunshine to face the battery of press and TV cameras feeling that the health service had been shown up. It had been an outstanding performance by Mr Milmo.

Barry picked Rhys up and held him in the air. 'Tomorrow my son will be delivering a petition against the closure of Westminster Hospital, signed by twenty-five thousand people, to the Prime Minister,' he said. But in the back of his mind he wondered where all this was leading. All he really wanted to do was get Rhys into a bone marrow transplant unit and start the treatment.

The next day, however, Barry was as good as his word and Rhys was knocking on the door of Number 10 Downing Street.

On 17 June they were back at the High Court to hear the judges' ruling. It was to be hailed as a victory by Barry and Carmen, their counsel Patrick Milmo and their solicitor Alan Meyer, who had become such a great friend and supporter of their cause.

The two London health authorities were criticised for breaching their statutory responsibilities in failing to ensure consultation procedures over the closure of Westminster's bone marrow transplant unit.

But Lord Justice Kennedy told Barry that he could not order the reopening of the unit or make a declaration that the authorities had acted unlawfully. He also rejected the argument that the closure of the unit in April amounted to a breach of duty by Virginia Bottomley. However, the judge said that uncertainty over the unit had been a tragedy for Rhys because it had delayed his treatment for Batten's disease by at least eight months.

The viability of the unit had come under scrutiny as it was not treating enough patients and the health authorities – Riverside and North-West Thames – entered negotiations with Guy's Hospital, Great Ormond Street and Hammersmith and Fulham Hospital with a view to a merger. However, the health authorities failed to consult Riverside Community Health Council, the body legally entrusted to oversee health-care provision, as they were statutorily obliged to do when varying services.

Lord Justice Kennedy said that even when the council got wind of what was happening and requested information, it had difficulty obtaining a reply. Then it got a letter which was significant in failing to reveal the extent to which the unit had already been allowed to fade away.

Outside the court in the sunshine Rhys stood in front of the cameras and rubbed his tired eyes.

'The judgement was excellent,' Barry told newsmen. 'The judge basically said that the closure was a shambles. He went along with us on most of the points that we made.'

North-West Thames Regional Health Authority accepted the judgement and said: 'We very much regret the distress caused to the Daniels family.'

Shadow Health Secretary David Blunkett said: 'Mrs Bottomley should now act to restore children's bone marrow services in the south of England.'

The next day Barry was airborne again – this time on his way to Abuja, Nigeria, via Lagos, for his company. It was a nightmare trip and he could almost smell the corruption the second he put foot on Nigerian soil. He got caught up in political riots in the city and on his return was mugged by security and army staff at Lagos airport.

The hotel Eko Merdian had a computer problem. Barry soon realised what it was, but he could only sort it out if he returned to Britain to order, and then pick up, the electronic parts, flown in from America. Then he would have to check them to make sure they were exactly right because of the costs involved.

Barry explained the situation to the hotel manager who wasn't impressed.

'Your passport has been confiscated,' he said. 'You will not be allowed to leave until you have solved our little problem.'

Barry explained the situation carefully, slowly, painstakingly again. The two men were leaning over the reception desk staring at each other. Barry could tell they would never hit it off.

'Did you know that it only costs fifty dollars to have someone – how do you English say? – "taken out" in this town?' said the manager.

Barry got the message. Within minutes he was on the telephone trying to ring the British Embassy from his hotel room. Strange, but he couldn't get through. Finally, he managed to get through to his brother David in England. David, realising the danger, immediately began diplomatic negotiations with the hotel for Barry's release. He had been advised by the Foreign Office in London how volatile the area was and he was trying to be calm and patient. But by now Barry wasn't showing any diplomacy at all. He told the hotel manager just what he thought of him, although some of the four-letter words didn't seem to register. Finally, after a few days, a deal was sorted out and his passport was handed over – just five minutes before Barry left for the bus to catch his scheduled flight home. The hotel manager bid him farewell, reminding Barry that he had friends in the army at the airport.

Barry was convinced he would be the next kidnap victim on the BBC News.

But the nightmare did not end there. When he caught the courtesy bus to the airport, he found himself the only passenger. The three officials riding with him demanded $50 before they let him off. Barry had no alternative but to hand over the cash. He had just $20 left. At the check-in a uniformed official, surrounded by soldiers brandishing machine guns, took his passport, ticket and luggage – then demanded $100 to let him on the plane.

'But I haven't got a hundred dollars,' said Barry.

'Then you haven't got a plane,' said the official, smiling sarcastically.

'But you've got my ticket – and my luggage!'

'What ticket – what luggage?'

'The ticket I just bloody well gave you!'

Barry heard the click of a machine-gun catch.

'One hundred dollars,' the official repeated.

For a moment, Barry didn't care if he was gunned to death on the spot. It was a state of mind he had picked up in Los Angeles all those years ago. What would be, would be. He began to swear and shout and the soldiers moved towards him. Then he remembered Rhys, Charly and Carmen. He had to get home, but the situation looked bleak – no ticket, no passport, no luggage, no money, no Epping. He pulled out his last $20 note.

'Look, this is all I have. Please let me catch the plane.'

After what seemed like an eternity, the official appeared to believe him and let him through.

The plane looked and felt like it was held together with rubber bands, but the flight home was the best thing that had happened to him for days.

136

When he was airborne Barry looked down at the city.

'I won't be coming back for a holiday, boys,' he said under his breath.

But in England there was good news waiting for him. Dr Jackie Cornish rang from Bristol. A perfect match donor had been found for Rhys — and the ethical board had given the final go-ahead.

'I hate you!' Carmen screamed. Barry stood in the middle of the disco floor, beer dripping down his face on to his shirt as Carmen ran out. It was a violent end to another fund-raising karaoke evening. A crowd gathered around the door of the village hall watching Barry chase Carmen into the night.

The hot summer evening had started with a swing. There was no bar at the hall in the village of Thornwood, Essex, so everyone had taken their own drinks. Barry's friends Rick and Linda, over from America for the occasion, joined in the singing and dancing. Everyone was having fun and it was just like a school reunion for Barry. It was the first time he had seen so many classmates since he had left Epping Comprehensive. Carmen drank one glass of wine after another, each one dulling the painful memories of the last six months. She began to unwind, putting the thought of Rhys's treatment about to start in Bristol, out of her mind. But she wasn't herself, she couldn't really let herself go, couldn't really enjoy the occasion as much as she wanted to. The stress had built up to a level she could hardly control. All the worries, the uncertainties and fears were bubbling over.

It was 10.30 p.m. when she finished the last dregs of the wine bottle with her friend Emma and looked over at Barry as the slow music came on. It was as if a

137

trigger had gone off in her mind. He was dancing close with a pretty girl. Emma was speaking to Carmen and she was answering, but she wasn't listening properly. Emma's words were a distant echo.

When the music stopped, Barry sat down chatting to his friend Ray about music and guitars and groups and . . . Carmen, seething with silent anger, beckoned to him with her index finger.

As he approached the table where she was standing, something snapped inside her and the pent-up emotions of the past months gushed out. She picked up a pint glass of beer and threw it over him.

Barry stood for a moment deeply shocked as she turned and ran, ran out of the club into the clean, fresh air, scarcely knowing where she was running to until she found herself in the road leading down to the old cottages. She just wanted to run away from everybody, her life, her kids even. She just wanted to run off the edge of the world and disappear.

Barry caught up with her and grabbed her arm. She screamed and kicked and punched him as he held on. All she could see was the pretty young girl in his arms. One of her friends was crying and screaming in the background.

'Carmen, for God's sake, calm down!' Barry shouted.

She sunk her teeth deep into his hand and he let go. She ran on again, but he caught her up and brought her to the ground.

'Don't be stupid. Stop it, Carmen. Calm down!'

The police car slowly rolled to a halt beside them and the two officers got out.

It was an embarrassing moment. They asked Carmen if she was all right and, still shaking with rage, she assured them that she was as Barry stood looking like some sort of beast in the night. When they offered to take her home she agreed.

'But he's not coming,' she said, pointing at her ashen-faced husband who was looking even more guilty than before. Barry stood and watched the police car speed away as the officers drove Carmen back to the hall to pick up her bag and keys and her friend Emma. While she was getting her things, one of the guests poked her head into the car and said: 'You do know who that is, don't you? It's Carmen Daniels. We've been raising money for the Charly and Rhys Appeal.'

It was Carmen's first time in a police car and she felt like she was appearing before the Spanish Inquisition.

'How long have you been married?' one of the officers asked. 'Do you row often? Is your husband volatile? How many children do you have? Will you be all right at home? Is your friend staying the night with you?'

Carmen and Emma had been in the house about five minutes when the crew arrived. She opened the door to a worried-looking Barry and Rick and Linda and the rest . . . and seconds later they all burst out laughing. What a great introduction to the English way of life for their American guests.

Barry and Carmen put their luggage in the little hallway of the flat that had been provided for them by Mr Al Fayed in the grounds of Bristol University and Rhys ran around the large lounge.

'We'll need a washing machine,' said Carmen, looking around the kitchen, 'and a Hoover and a . . .'

Barry picked up the telephone and rang Dingle's department store in the town asking for the manager just as the Harrods chairman had told him to. By the end of the day everything needed for their stay near Bristol's Royal Hospital for Sick Children had been delivered.

The Bristol unit specialised in bone marrow transplants, but its biggest problem was lack of space and facilities. Nevertheless, they were prepared for Rhys.

'Somehow we manage to get all the children on our waiting list transplanted in time, but it gives us lots of heartache and difficulty,' Dr Jackie Cornish told a reporter over the telephone. The press was hungry for more details.

'We have to decide which child is given priority. That is a pressure we should not have to cope with. A bone marrow transplant is the end of the line for most children. A few years ago, it wasn't always possible to find a suitable donor, but now we can find them for over 90 per cent of our patients. This is mainly because children can cope well with mismatched donors – adults can't. Our biggest problem is finding the beds to treat the youngsters.'

Since the unit opened in 1987, it had done 200 transplants – nearly half using unrelated donors.

But things were looking up. Plans were under way to move into a new super unit, purpose-built to cope with 100 transplants a year. Ten isolation cubicles were planned, a spacious ward, a luxurious playroom and a separate outpatients' department.

The million-pound, self-contained unit was being paid for by the hospital and the Cogent Trust based at Westminster Children's Hospital until it closed down.

Thanks to the Cogent cash the unit would soon be able to specialise in bone marrow transplants for metabolic and genetic diseases as well as leukaemia. Four out of five children with such rare and deadly illnesses, whose only chance of life was a transplant, had no matching family donor.

The new unit would soon turn Bristol into the biggest children's transplant centre outside America. But there still wasn't enough money to provide the equipment. It would remain an empty shell unless the money could be raised to buy the drips, monitors and machines needed to offer the chance of survival to children like Rhys.

The charity Children With Leukaemia was battling to collect enough cash to provide much of the early equipment.

'Yes, you're right. It is a sign of the times that in order to give a service to the degree of excellence we want, we have to go out and raise the money,' Dr Cornish told the reporter.

She put down the telephone, turned and smiled at Barry and Carmen.

'Now then,' she said. 'Let's talk about Rhys.'

Barry couldn't believe his eyes when he read the headline in the local newspaper. His great friend Rose Patterson, who had worked with him on the recording of 'Love's So Hard', had been killed in a horrific car accident. From that morning on, he would never be able to listen to the song again without a tear coming to his eye.

'Come on, Rhys. You have to take the medicine. If you don't, you'll get wobbly legs like Charly,' said Barry, coaxing his son to swallow the red and white and orange pills.

Rhys reluctantly gulped them down as Barry and Carmen sat on his bed watching another combination of drugs flow into his body through the Hickman line attached to his chest. They were both scared, bloody scared. This had been their decision and theirs alone. If anything went wrong, they bore the responsibility.

The doctors at Bristol were beginning to fine-tune Rhys's immune system with medication, so that it would be ready to take the implant of new bone marrow. But it was a risk. His body would be open to other infections, even a cold could have life-threatening effects. It was hell for Carmen to watch her joyful, bouncy, healthy two-year-old son being sick from the effects of drugs and chemotherapy, trying to make him understand it was all for his own good.

Barry sat on the bed fiddling with the toy space gun, remembering what the nurse had told him. The weeks of conditioning drugs and chemotherapy administered before the three-hour transplant was just like taking your body to the brink of death and praying you had the strength to come back again, she said. He hadn't told Carmen.

When Rhys fell asleep, they walked back to the flat arm in arm, not speaking, just thinking and looking, looking at the passers-by. They all seemed so serious, so lost in thought, as if they had all the troubles of the world on their shoulders. Carmen wondered what those troubles could be – paying their mortgages, a love affair that had ended, a broken washing machine, a car that wouldn't start? She wondered if they would like to swap their troubles for hers.

They walked up the two flights of stairs in the old Victorian house to the flat Mr Al Fayed had rented for them. The view from the lounge window was wonderful: they could see right across the Mendip Hills. It was a warm, sunny evening and the clear blue sky was full of hot air balloons of every shape, colour and size. They stood for a moment staring at the scene.

'Perhaps we should all fly away in a balloon, you,

Charly, Rhys and I,' said Barry.

'Yes, perhaps we should,' said Carmen. 'Perhaps we should fly off to a different solar system to find the God who packed his bags and left us all, just like you told me before.'

The ring of the telephone interrupted their fantasy. It was another reporter. Barry drew a deep breath and was as polite as he could be. He was tired now . . . and tired of answering the same old questions.

'No, the donor isn't related. No, we don't know who he or she is. The person wants to stay anonymous. Yes, a brother or sister would normally be used as the bone marrow donor in such a case, but this was not an option for Rhys because his sister Charly also has the disease. Yes, using a donor outside the family unfortunately adds to the risk, but we are prepared to take it – and so is the hospital. Thank you. Goodbye.'

Barry checked on Charly, who was asleep in the bedroom. She seemed to be settling in OK in her new home in Bristol, not really understanding why they were all there and what all the commotion was about. Barry tucked her in. Bless her heart, he thought. Why was life such a bitch?

The press had been hot on their trail all through Rhys's treatment. Barry and Carmen tried to please them all and seemed to manage quite well, but at times it was overpowering.

Barry turned on the TV to watch the news. Rhys was the top news story on the BBC and ITN.

The telephone rang and Barry sighed, thinking it was another reporter. But this time it was Carmen's friend, Jacky Crump.

'What's wrong?' asked Barry, squeezing the hot tea-bag with a spoon as Carmen came into the kitchen a few minutes later.

'It's Alison. Jacky says they think she has got liver cancer.'

In January 1991, Charly had started playschool. As the weeks went on Carmen became friendly with two other mothers. One of them was Alison Hack, who had two daughters, Gemma and Joanna, and a son, James. The other, Jacky, had a little girl named Stacey and a son, Simon. Both Gemma and Stacey were slightly older than Charly and appointed themselves as her guardian angels. Charly was forever falling over or bumping against things and they were always on hand to pick up the pieces or keep a watchful eye on her.

Jacky, Alison and Carmen would get together once a week for a coffee and a chat. Alison had been a nurse at Great Ormond Street and when Charly was diagnosed as having Batten's disease she proved to be a tower of strength for Barry and Carmen, always on hand to lend a sympathetic ear or shoulder to cry on. She was the most unselfish person Carmen knew. Even though she had three children of her own to look after she would take Charly any time to give Carmen and Barry a break. She even swapped her car for a big estate to ferry Charly and her own children around.

'I've got to go and see her,' said Carmen.

'Of course, we'll all be OK,' said Barry.

The next morning as Carmen drove down to London and back to Epping she reflected on her life. For Charly the clock was running backwards. In just two years Carmen had watched her waste away from a pretty, little laughing girl to a five-year-old with the mental age of under one.

Within twelve months or so Carmen knew she would have to feed her by tube as she lost the power to swallow and eventually she would have to make a decision to unplug her life-support machine.

When Carmen realised that she was going to lose Charly, she swore to make each day the best it could be for her. At this moment Charly was still fairly aware, could sit up and had some sight.

How unfair could life be? Charly had been a normal, three-year-old who had learned to walk and talk. She was active, curious and irresistible. Suddenly and without warning she became sick with a variety of symptoms that were difficult to explain – seizures, convulsions. Soon she would be a complete invalid.

'God, my own daughter, my own precious daughter! Why not take me – take me!'

Carmen stopped at the traffic lights and looked around to see if anyone had seen her shouting out loud to herself. She was full of mixed emotions about Alison, about Charly and Rhys, Barry's father even.

She watched the young boy carrying the guitar case stroll across the road, as if he had all the time in the world. She wished she had all the time in the world too. How wonderful it would be to soak in a bath with a glass of champagne and go out for an evening free from worrying that everything was all right at home. How wonderful it would be to pamper herself and stay in bed when she had a cold or felt unwell. She looked at her tired eyes in the windscreen mirror and saw shadows under them from sitting up late at night with Rhys. The young boy crossing the road reminded her of Barry. He had given up his musical hopes and aspirations after Charly was born to get a more stable job and provide a good home. Now he was expressing himself in his writing again – in that respect he was lucky. Carmen wished she could sing, or write or something, get it all out of her, all the gnawing, sad feelings.

She pulled away from the traffic lights and sang the words of Barry's song, thinking of Charly:

I promise I will fill your days with all the joys of life,
And bring you happiness, through the sadness that we
  hide.
Love will last forever. No one can take that away,
But you can't begin to measure when life's the price you
  pay.
It tears my emotions back where we begun,
Can life be so cruel to those so young?

Carmen had to bite her lip to stop herself from crying. She couldn't believe what had happened to her friend, how she had changed, how thin she looked lying in the hospital bed, how yellow she was. As she and Jacky walked back to the car park at Holly House Hospital, Buckhurst Hill, Essex, they couldn't hold in their tears any more. They cried and cried and hugged and hugged.

But Alison never gave up. She began a course of chemotherapy and weeks later took her children to school. That was Alison, always joking and ringing to find out how Charly and Rhys were.

7: Heartbreak and Hope

The Hospital unit at Bristol was warm and friendly, run like a family concern. Everyone knew everyone, and the support for the worried and distressed parents was second to none. The centre had only four isolation units with a small pre-transplant ward containing three or four beds.

Barry and Carmen entered the second week of Rhys's treatment watching him begin to suffer the side effects of the drugs. He was vomiting and sweating and losing his hair. They could hardly bear it.

But it wasn't a depressing place. The little ward was painted colourfully. There were get-well cards all over the walls and the shelves were packed with presents from well-wishers. There was a small playroom at the end of the corridor stuffed full of toys and a colour TV. Children came in for follow-up treatment, nurses ran around with drugs and infusion pumps. There was never a dull moment.

It was hot, sticky summer weather. No windows could be opened in the ward because of the nature of the treatment and the need to keep a sterile atmosphere, so the constant hum of an electric fan buzzed around the place all day.

Barry and Carmen sat with Rhys around the clock, taking it in turns to go back to the flat to make sure Charly was happy and comfortable.

At this time Charly was doing OK. She was still fairly alert but unable to walk. She could only say a couple of words and her eyesight was failing. She had no idea why Barry and Carmen were setting up home hundreds of miles away from the old one. She had very little understanding. The devastating disease was tightening its grip.

Carmen sat in front of the fire in the flat crying. It was the most moving letter she had ever read.

'I can't go on – you read it to me,' she said to Barry.

He took the American magazine from her and began to read aloud:

As I sit here on a snowy, Sunday afternoon, my mind is whirling with recent conversations, just as the snowflakes are whirling outside, like bits of lace or feathers on the wind. I know that I am safe and warm in my living room, enjoying the peaceful scene. But outside, there are travellers who are worried about making it to their destinations without slipping and sliding. I am so aware of seeing life situations from many angles and needing the ability to choose the best angle.

Right now, my daughter is asleep in her bed. She has a dry diaper, a full tummy and is cozy with her favourite teddy bears surrounding her. This is a contented, well cared for child. The realism of this view is that my daughter is eight years old but still needing a diaper. She has been fed an enriched-formula medicine and seizure control drugs through an external tube into

148

*a surgically-placed opening in her stomach. She is
propped into position with three bed pillows and her
teddy bears, because she cannot move. Music is coming
from a radio on her headboard, providing her with
auditory stimulation, one of her few remaining senses.*

Barry stopped for a moment and looked at Carmen.
He saw the tears in her eyes.

'Do you still want me to go on?'

'You know I do.'

Barry paused for a moment and then continued.
Somehow the letter was giving him comfort:

*My eight-year-old daughter is sleeping on a beautiful,
snowy Sunday afternoon because she is dying from a
rare genetic illness called Batten's disease. I don't see a
diseased, dying child. I only see my beautiful Laura
sleeping peacefully.*

I watched a TV show last night called Sisters. *I
enjoy this show because I have two sisters that I love
very much and although we aren't like the sisters on
TV, we were and still are great friends. In this
particular show, the older sister finds a lump in her
breast. The show dealt with the trauma of testing,
making decisions and dealing with the outcome. The
younger sister faced these kinds of decisions several
years ago when her son fought leukemia. Although her
son's outcome was successful, I felt that the writers
presented the issue with the understanding of what
families have to go through in the face of a sometimes
fatal disease.*

*Anyway, this sister is now faced with going through
such an ordeal with her older sister. Her belief in God
has been so stretched that she is having a difficult time
with the simple comments . . . God will take care of this,
put your faith in God and it is in God's hands now.*

The younger sister and her mother had a major disagreement when the mother suggested that they go to the hospital chapel to say a prayer. She was angry when she said that she felt it was unfair to sit and wait for God to dole out whatever he felt. In other words, enough is enough. The scene ended with the two women outside the hospital discussing their feelings. The daughter felt guilty about scorning her faith, but the mother said something very wise: without your faith, life would be very lonely.

Faith is what keeps us seeing the many facets of life. We have to deal with the everyday realism in order to survive. But we can also see the other sides that are created. Hidden blessings are a reality, and with these, we can endure anything.

Many people comment to me that they just don't know how I deal with Laura's care. I feel that I am being her mum and nothing more. If she were a talented musician, I would be providing her with the best teachers and instruments that money could buy. If she were showing signs of being an artist, same thing. If she wanted to be a rocket scientist or a computer genius, I would turn her over to her dad. Whatever it took to encourage her potential.

As it is, my daughter needs me for simple comforts which I have learned to provide. I am not a saint or a martyr, I am just her mum.

A cartoon I saw in today's newspaper brought this thinking to a head. Illustrated are two cavemen sitting on rocks talking. The first one says: 'I believe we were put here for a purpose.' His friend replies: 'Nonsense, we're here simply because we survived.' The first one asks: 'Survived what?'

'Why the Big Swamp, of course,' his friend answers.

'You think we came out of a swamp?' asks the first.

'Certainly!' says his friend. 'Look around you — nothing but slimeballs.'

The first man thinks: 'Now that you mention it . . .' But he adds, 'OK, how do you explain love?'

His friend ends this with: 'Give it up kid — if we aren't here to survive, we wouldn't have survived to be here.'

We all have the ability to survive: it is just how we use that ability. The saying God only gives as much as you can handle isn't really a comforting thought.

If this were true, there probably wouldn't be any suicides.

I don't want to believe that there was a decision made that I could handle the premature death of my daughter, that I don't get to see her accomplish her goals and dreams, and not to enjoy having grandchildren some day.

What I do believe is, I have the faith that can see me through the hardest days of my life and the ability to survive. After all, I am not the first mum to have a child with Batten's disease and, I am sorry to say, I am not the last.

Life is a constant challenge of making choices. You may have a sad time in your life, but you don't have to live sad. It does take more energy at times to look for the silver lining, but once you see it, it will help you to accept your task at hand.

Barry sat staring at the newsletter for a moment and Carmen looked into the fire. They didn't speak for what seemed like an eternity, both understanding the strength that Laura's mother had found in her own faith.

151

Finally, Carmen turned and said: 'What a wonderful woman.'

'Yes, wonderful,' Barry replied.

They were to share many thoughts and feelings with Laura's mother from then on.

The doctors were amazed. It was just 48 hours since the transplant and Rhys was tucking into baked beans on toast as if he hadn't eaten for weeks. Normally, an infusion of bone marrow left the patient tired and debilitated. The signs were good but Barry and Carmen knew that ahead of him lay a long spell in isolation with just a few of his favourite toys for company.

That morning *The Times* had run a big colour picture of Rhys tucked up in bed with his favourite Mickey Mouse doll.

Each time Barry and Carmen visited him they had to wear surgical gowns and pass through sterile chambers before they got to his isolation cubicle. Even Rhys's toys had to be spotless and germ-free before he could play with them in his room.

Rhys was in isolation cubicle number four, Barry and Carmen's favourite. One of the large windows looked out on to the nurse's station which was always busy. It provided good entertainment value. They could watch all the daily goings-on which was a bonus because the world of isolation was unbelievably quiet. Another large window looked out over the baby unit on to the huge Bristol University building that was like a castle tower. Rhys thought that Beauty and the Beast lived there, and he was fascinated by the spires.

Slowly, over the next few weeks, he got stronger, running around his isolation unit still attached to the machines that monitored his condition day by day, hour by hour, minute by minute.

Dawn was Rhys's favourite nurse. She was a fiery little lady with a bubbly personality. There were lots of laughs and jokes and they all formed a strong friendship. Barry and Carmen felt that she was part of their family. Dr Oakhill would come round the ward and press his face up against Rhys's window. To Rhys, Dr Tony, as he was called, was the best thing that ever happened. He lit up whenever Dr Tony was around. He would draw animals on Rhys's window, until after about a week in isolation the window was covered with drawings and scribbles.

Rhys seemed to have come through the transplant with flying colours. But Dr Oakhill had told Barry and Carmen that he would get sick before he got better. They sat and waited. But Rhys just got better and stronger every day. Dr Oakhill was totally astonished one morning to look through the glass and see Rhys bouncing up and down on a trampoline.

By now Charly was attending a local school in Bristol – the Claremont Special School – where she made some really good friends and was well looked after. With the help of an *Evening Standard* appeal, Barry was able to hire a private special-needs nurse to look after her when the school finally closed for the summer. Her name was Caroline Hurley, a student who had just finished her studies and special-needs training. They hit it off right from the start and Caroline took Charly all over Bristol, which gave Barry and Carmen more time with Rhys.

And then came the best news of all – home leave. Rhys was to be let out of hospital to spend a few hours with Barry and Carmen at the flat – but it was crucial that he was kept away from other people because of the risk of infection, and it could still be a year before doctors knew if the transplant had been successful. A year of hope and worry for Carmen.

Barry bought Rhys, now completely bald, a blue and yellow baseball cap which he wore back to front just like a rock star. It stopped him stroking his head and wondering why he didn't have any hair.

'Things are on the up,' Barry told reporters who rang him on his sacred mobile telephone. 'So far, there have been no complications. We are thrilled that Rhys is out of hospital, if only for a few hours. It has been a long, hard road just to get this far. But in my heart I always knew we would make it.'

'What's for tea, mum – I'm coming home!' said Rhys, clutching Barry's mobile telephone.

It was all over – for the time being. It was 13 September 1993 and the cameras clicked and reporters cheered on the steps of the hospital. Transplant Sister Jane Cahill gave Rhys a hug and Barry told the newsmen: 'We're just so glad everything has turned out well and we can take him back home to Epping. The doctors are pleased with how Rhys is doing, but it's going to be a few months yet until we know if the operation has been a success. I'd just like to thank all the nurses for their help. They've been wonderful.

'At first Rhys was a bit scared, but after a while he settled down and soon got to know all the staff by their names. And, of course, we'd like to thank the donor who we still don't know. Without him or her, Rhys would not have had the life-saving treatment.

'We haven't got anything special planned tonight, just a nice, quiet reunion with all the family and friends.'

Carmen watched the news broadcast on TV, sitting

cuddling Charly. 'Rhys is coming home for a hug today,' she said. But Charly didn't hear her. It was 10.00 in the morning and she was in a deep sleep, lost in her own little world. Carmen wondered what sort of world it was. If only she could get in there with her too.

Carmen walked into the chemist shop and bought a pregnancy kit, her mind racing. Was she really expecting another baby? What would Barry say? What would the world say?

Her period was late, but just by one week. In any other woman such a fact would be partially ignored. But it couldn't be with Carmen. She had to know now. The only thing she knew was that she and Barry believed in their hearts that whatever happened with Charly and Rhys they still wanted a family. No one could change their minds about that, or take away the hope that one day everything would be all right. Professor Lake had told them in Hamburg about pre-natal testing and that the rate of detecting the defective Batten's cells at sixteen weeks was around 90 per cent accurate. Surely they had a chance. They hadn't planned this but they both felt joy and apprehension.

'What will we tell the family?' asked Carmen.

'Just the truth,' said Barry. 'There will be mixed reactions.'

He was right. When they told the family some were really pleased. Others showed their dissent.

'Haven't you got enough to cope with? What did you want to do that for?' one of them said over the telephone. Others too were dismayed.

Barry and Carmen understood them, but they didn't understand Barry and Carmen. This was the position they were now in – and they had been told that not every child they had would suffer from Batten's disease. The tears flowed again. Couldn't they do anything right?

The evening shadows danced around the bedroom. Barry watched them moving from the wall to the floor, to the ceiling and back to the curtains. Carmen stared at the ceiling questioning everyone to herself: 'What are you all waiting for? Charly to die, maybe? You wouldn't have all worried if our kids were normal. What does the world expect from us?'

In the hospital the next day, Carmen kissed her grandfather goodbye.

'Give my babies a kiss for me,' he muttered under his breath.

Gran, as he was affectionately nicknamed, had undergone a hip replacement operation. But he had picked up a bad stomach bug and was poorly. He had always suffered with emphysema, asthma and bronchitis and now his ill health was telling. The family were sitting around the bed drinking tea and eating ham rolls and he was semi-conscious. He had always been one of Carmen's favourite people, always shown her love and understanding. Carmen waved as she left the ward. It was the last time she would ever see him. He died shortly after midnight the following evening.

The next day, heartbroken as she was, she and Barry had to take Rhys for a check-up. But it was Carmen who ended up in hospital. She had started to bleed and suffered terrible stomach cramps. She underwent an ultrasound scan and an hour later she and Barry were called into the doctor's office.

'I have some very bad news,' she said. 'The baby has aborted.'

'OK, fine,' said Carmen, calmly. 'I suppose this miscarriage is nothing compared to what we've got to go through with our two other children.'

The doctor just stared and said: 'I guess not.'

Carmen was admitted to the hospital and around ten o'clock that night was wheeled into the theatre for a D and C.

All she could think about now was being well enough to attend Gran's funeral.

'Hello, is that Barry Daniels?'

'Yes.'

'It's Julia Morley here, Chief Barker of the Variety Club.'

'Oh, hello. Yes, I know who you are. You did the Miss World contests didn't you?'

'That's right. But do you know all about the Variety Club of Great Britain, or rather Tent 36, as it is formally known?'

Julia had read Rhys's story in the national newspapers and with her husband, millionaire businessman Eric Morley, had seen him on TV.

'I want to send you all to Give Kids the World,' she said.

Give Kids the World was an organisation that gave children with life-threatening diseases a holiday of a lifetime at a specially built village near Orlando, the Florida home of Disneyworld. It worked with over 240 foundations, charities and hospitals in 30 countries in fulfilling a child's last wish to see Mickey Mouse.

The 35 acres that brought so much happiness to handicapped and under-privileged children was the creation of hotelier Henri Landwirth. Every year he welcomed 4,000 youngsters and parents to his magical wonderland.

157

Situated on the shores of a lake, 56 specially designed, two-bedroom villas offered all the comforts of home – TVs, videos and fully stocked kitchens. They were filled with people who had one thing in common. They were bonded together because their children were ill or under-privileged. All the children and their parents were met at the airport, where they received gifts, complimentary meals at top restaurants and tickets to Disneyworld and other theme parks. At the village itself there was a gingerbread house, restaurant, a beautiful chapel, a caboose, a castle filled with toys and games, a real fire engine, plane and a pirate ship pier.

Henri, who considered everyone as a guest, knew all about the harsher facts of life. Born the son of a diamond-cutter in Antwerp, as a boy of thirteen he had been sent to Auschwitz, one of the most notorious death camps set up by the Nazis during the Second World War. He survived the Holocaust and later settled in America where he built a successful hotel business and launched a youth charity in memory of his mother.

But it was one particular little English girl who inspired Give Kids the World.

In 1986, when he was working hard building up his company and his fortune, he got many letters and telephone calls from people who needed help. He would do what he could, but sometimes he was too busy to deal personally with them all.

Then he received a letter from a little English girl who was suffering from leukaemia. She had always wanted to see America and Mickey Mouse and Donald Duck. Henri agreed to help, but business commitments held him up, there were so many other things to do. Finally, he got around to making the arrangements. But it was too late. The little girl had died. From that moment on Henri swore he would never let a child wait again. He was filled with sadness and so he built Give Kids the World.

His motto became:

We make a living by what we get, but we make a life by what we give.

Barry was thinking about the trip to Florida when he came home from work. He got the usual crazy greeting from Rhys who threw himself into his father's arms and pointed to toys and tried to shoot water from an empty waterpistol at Charly lying on the sofa.

Barry put Rhys down and went over to the sofa and gave Charly a hug. She had been very quiet recently, much quieter than usual.

Suddenly, out of the blue, she said: 'Daddy.'

Barry broke down and cried. She hadn't said that word for months.

The last word she had ever said to him was 'Muffin', the name of Carmen's mother's cross-bred terrier she had loved so much.

A few days later they took Charly to see Mohamed Al Fayed's eye specialist in Harley Street. After tests she was registered blind, but the doctor told them she still had some slight vision – light and dark. They felt that another piece of Charly had been taken away.

Carmen stood alone, quietly sobbing in the bedroom so that Charly and Rhys wouldn't hear her. Her dear friend from Charly's playschool, Alison, had died of liver cancer in a hospice. Her last wish had been granted – that her beloved children were not brought to see her. She wanted them to remember her the way she used to be.

Shortly before she died, she and her husband Richard had taken their children to Euro Disney for one last memorable holiday. Richard had made a video of the occasion for the family to keep for ever. But Carmen could never bring herself to see it.

At the funeral there wasn't a dry eye in the church for the wonderful lady who had been Charly's guardian angel.

Carmen walked home through the January rain, across the park dotted with shiny, grey puddles. Her friend was at peace now. At least Charly would have someone to watch over her for ever. Somehow Carmen took great comfort in that thought.

Julia Morley saw Barry, Carmen, Rhys and Charly off at Gatwick airport on 31 January. The whole itinerary had been kept simple. Charly was having difficulty with her sight and was beginning to feel uncomfortable anywhere else but at home. But they had a wonderful time in the land of magic and Mickey Mouse.

Barry would grab a towel from the bathroom each morning, put a shirt over his boxer shorts and run down to the pool carrying Charly. He would make her comfortable in a chair and dive in relishing the shock of the clear blue water, flipping on to his back to watch the sun begin to climb in the sky. Then he would gently take her in too, splashing the water against her feet at first to make her aware of the temperature. Then they would float around as he told her about the rides they would be going on in Disneyworld later that day.

The date – 10 February – would stay forever embedded in Carmen's mind. She had wondered more than once over the last few days if Rhys was all right, if his new bone marrow was working. She had been looking for signs that it wasn't and one morning, when she saw his legs wobble, she was sure the surgery had failed and the disease that had such a grip on her daughter now had its long, cruel fingers around her son too. But the doctor told her it was just the drugs Rhys was taking.

It was just turned half past seven when they headed off in the car for Bristol. There was an icy wind and Carmen huddled down inside her coat keeping her hands in her pockets until the car heater warmed up. Barry didn't talk much, he just drove.

Dr Tony Oakhill and Dr Jackie Cornish had called a special meeting to discuss Rhys. Barry and Carmen both feared the worst, although they didn't admit it to each other.

'I'm sorry you two, but I'm afraid it's bad news.'

Barry bit on the top of his lip and Carmen squeezed her wedding ring. Jackie was visibly upset as Dr Oakhill continued: 'All the tests now show that the transplant hasn't worked. Rhys's body has rejected the bone marrow.'

Barry felt cheated. He and Carmen had put Rhys through it all for nothing. All that sickness he had suffered. Suddenly their lives were empty. All the fighting, all the heartbreak, all the pain. For what? To sit in this little room and realise it had meant nothing. All that time Rhys had been bounding around his little isolation unit and jumping up and down on his trampoline, his body had been killing off the new bone marrow cells. What the hell should they do now?

As soon as the news broke in Britain the search was on for a new donor and Queen guitarist Brian May became involved.

Brian was the patron of the British Bone Marrow Donor Appeal. 'I have seen too many children die because a donor could not be found in time for them,' he told the press. 'I could not bear to see another child die and I want everyone to do what they can to help us save Rhys. We will move heaven and earth to find a donor for him. Barry and his wife Carmen are going through hell. Time has already nearly run out for Charly and now they could lose Rhys as well. We can't allow time to run out for him too.'

Brian underwent tests to see if he could be a match for Rhys but he wasn't. The DNA of only one person in 40,000 would be compatible.

Late in February, Barry received a telephone call from Malcolm Thomas, one of the founders of the British Bone Marrow Donor Appeal. He too wanted to do all he could for Rhys. He more than most was aware of the heartache and uphill struggle Barry and Carmen had faced. He had lost his daughter Alexandra to a condition called aplastic anaemia because a donor could not be found in time for her. Since that heartbreaking day he had helped hundreds of children through his sheer determination not to let any situation beat him.

The British Bone Marrow Donor Appeal was founded in August 1987 by Malcolm and another father, John Humphries. No donor could be found for John's son Mark either, but Mark had battled his way through leukaemia with intensive treatment and the disease had finally gone into remission. During the search for donors for their children, Malcolm and John discovered that time didn't wait for victims of such tragic diseases. The clock often ran out before the two vital tests necessary to match an unrelated donor with a patient could be completed. The two fathers got together and came up with the idea to speed up the distressing process by doing both tests together. They approached the National Blood Transfusion Service to see if this was possible and the Service agreed to help. Its blood donor centres could do all the tests for blood and bone marrow at the same time. Malcolm and John then launched their British Bone Marrow Donor Appeal to raise money to pay for the tests and the extra equipment needed in the blood transfusion centres. Their aim was to build a register of 100,000 potential donors and for the first time a charity began to work hand in hand with the National Health Service.

Soon the results of their work became known nationwide as children's lives began to be saved. Children like little Ben Jones from Swansea, Wales, who made front-page news. Ben was born with the rare bone marrow disease Wiscott Aldrich. When he was just a few months old his parents were told that only a bone marrow transplant could save him. A donor was found on the British Bone Marrow Donor Appeal register and soon after his first birthday Ben had the transplant which saved his life.

The courageous campaign of leukaemia-victim Denise Morse raised nearly £1 million for the Appeal. Denise, from Stoke on Trent, knew it was too late for a bone marrow transplant to save her, but she spent the last six months of her life raising money for the fund so that others would be saved. 'I want to help so that other people with leukaemia don't have to die,' she told the nation. Denise died, aged 33, in February 1989, but not before her amazing fight to help others had touched the hearts of millions. Her courage and strength would never be forgotten and many bone marrow disease victims in the future would owe their lives to her.

Rock star May joined the Appeal after reading about Denise's bravery. He even released a new version of the Queen hit record 'Who Wants To Live Forever', after hearing that it was her favourite song and was played at her funeral. The record raised £100,000 for the cause.

By now Barry and Carmen were beginning to understand a lot of things. There were hundreds of other families just like them who needed help. Thousands, even. They needed a place to stay when they had to travel long distances to get treatment, they needed help with finances, they needed advice . . . and there just weren't enough donors for all the children who desperately needed transplants.

Through people like Malcolm and Tony Moreland of the Anthony Nolan Bone Marrow Appeal, Barry and Carmen began to realise that up until Charly was diagnosed they had taken things for granted. Now they knew that the greatest gift of all was the gift of life – and you could never thank someone enough for trying to give your child that gift.

A few days later Barry and Carmen appeared on TV on *Kilroy*. The subject was bone marrow transplants and the need for government funding for the donor appeals. It was a lively debate, well chaired by presenter Robert Kilroy Silk.

The families taking part made it an emotional occasion and Barry and Carmen left feeling they had, in some small way, done something to bring awareness of the problems to the attention of the country. But somehow it wasn't enough. Now they wanted to do more – but what?

Soon Barry was globe-trotting again. This time he was off to the International Batten's Disease Conference in New York where Professor Brian Lake was doing a presentation on Rhys's transplant and the subsequent findings.

The audience was fascinated. The professor couldn't find anything in the tests carried out after the bone marrow implant to say that it would work. But equally there was not enough evidence to say it wouldn't work either. There were slides and a lot of technical data for the scientists to study, but they made no sense to Barry. Whilst in America Barry made contact with his old friend Chris Sutton who was in New Jersey at the time. The day they spent together saw the combination of their musical skills once again, only this time to add some finishing touches to a very powerful ballad that Barry was writing for Charly called 'Little Girl Of Mine'.

'That's it, then. Definite?'

'Definite,' said Carmen.

They had made a difficult decision. Barry poured her another glass of wine and they sat watching the sun go down over the rooftops at the end of their garden. The rabbit was still out, bounding over wood chippings and toys in the play area. Barry watched the little creature make its way over the concrete slabs leading to the shed. It darted this way and that, not seeming to have any direction to go really. A bit like himself now.

After much soul searching they had finally decided not to go ahead with a second transplant for Rhys. They just couldn't put their little boy through it all again with no idea of the outcome.

Dr Oakhill understood when they told him at his office in Bristol. He was still very upset that things hadn't worked out better the first time.

'The choice is yours and naturally I respect your wishes,' he said.

165

The next few days seemed empty for them. There wasn't anything to aim for any more, no hope, nothing. They felt they were drowning in a tub of sticky blancmange. There was nothing to hold on to. They were just waiting . . . waiting for Rhys to show symptoms of Batten's disease.

Barry's Subaru estate car made its way through the greenery of Epping Forest. The woodland suddenly made way for houses, shops and the Duke of Wellington pub and Barry changed down a gear as he entered busy Epping High Street, smiling to himself that he and Carmen didn't have to shop at the sprawling red brick and glass Tesco store that evening. How he hated those supermarket trolleys. He could never get the pound coin in the metal locks that freed them from their chains and even when he did, he always seemed to take the trolley with squeaking wheels and a mind of its own. It would always insist on going left or right when he wanted to go straight down the aisle to the bread counter. Who designed those wheels anyway? He was sure he could do the job better.

Tonight was video and Chinese night. Special fried rice, sweet and sour pork and beef with black beans and chilli from the Wings Chinese takeaway restaurant and a Sharon Stone thriller from the Penny Farthing video rental shop.

Barry pulled up on his drive, grabbed his briefcase and went in the house to cuddle his kids, wondering if Carmen had got any beefburgers in the freezer for Charly because she hated Chinese food. He had only just stepped into the small hallway with its little wooden-framed mirror reflecting Charly on the sofa in the lounge when Carmen rushed up.

'We've raised enough money,' she shouted. 'Mr Al Fayed has offered to help!'

The Harrods boss had stepped in again and offered his help towards the cost of the family going to Amsterdam to see psychic Dean Kraft.

Barry had heard of Kraft's skills while watching satellite TV a month earlier in a 30-minute programme on the work of healers. From the second it began he was hooked. An hour later he was on the telephone to the film company Paramount in America to find out more about Kraft.

Charly, her beautiful blonde hair tied in a pony tail, could no longer speak. She had stopped walking eighteen months ago, only three years after taking her first faltering steps. Now she lay on the sofa staring blankly at the ceiling, her slender legs covered in pretty polka-dot leggings. Barry touched her face then walked across to the window. But her eyes didn't follow him as he looked out over the Herengracht, one of the most beautiful canals in central Amsterdam.

'This is beautiful, Charly,' he said. 'The canal is like a road. The houses sit right on it. They don't need cars here, Charly, only boats. It's like me coming home to you in a boat and not our car.'

Strangely, the building opposite had graffiti daubed on its walls. It was Barry's own initials, BPD. He wondered what they stood for.

He turned around. Charly couldn't even lift her head now. But he knew she could hear him.

'I know, I'll read to you from the tour book.'

Barry sat at his daughter's feet and flicked through the little green brochure.

'Here it is, the Herengracht,' he said, stroking her

little feet in their pink socks on top of the leggings. 'They call it the gentlemen's canal because it runs past some of the grandest merchant houses in the city. It was built in the seventeenth century.'

Charly's wide, blue eyes stared at him.

'OK, that's boring. Here are some fascinating facts then,' he said, turning from page to page. 'Did you know that Amsterdam has 540,000 bicycles for a population of 750,000, or that most of the alleyways and canals are named after flowers? Bet you didn't. And did you know there are 1,000 bridges and the whole city is built on huge pillars driven through the marshy ground to reach the hard earth below? Ah, here we are, you'll like this. This is what the Dutch eat. Breakfast is eggs, cheese, cold meat and jam and their favourite fish foods are herring, mackerel and eel.'

Barry looked at his daughter's eyes again, then leant over and gave her a kiss. He and Carmen were clutching at straws. Unconventional and expensive straws. Their daughter was now in nappies and cruelly dependent. She had the mental age of a twelve-week-old child and she was five. Barry held her hand for a moment then kissed it, his mind flashing images of her future. There wasn't one. There was no stopping the regression. It would continue until her sight failed completely. But perhaps there would be a miracle. A miracle brought to them by a psychic healer.

Barry had travelled to Amsterdam with Carmen, Charly and Rhys to seek the help of Dean Kraft. The trip was partly funded by the Charly and Rhys Appeal. Barry's cousin Julie was also on hand to help with the children as usual. They had heard so much about Kraft's powers that they just had to give it a try, but they knew that psychic healing and the laying on of

168

hands came without guarantees.

At around 11 a.m. Carmen returned to room 52 in the Amsterdam hotel with Rhys. They had been shopping, but she was tired and it was too cold to stay out any longer. She just wanted to sit for a while before Kraft arrived.

Rhys was full of life. He bustled around his motion-less sister, sometimes colliding with her pushchair, sometimes accidentally grabbing a handful of her pretty long, blonde hair as he stumbled. Then he would stop to kiss her and whisper 'Sorry' in her ear. To him Charly had always been an immobile figure who needed constant care. What he didn't know was that without some kind of miracle he too would start the slow crumble into neurological decline.

'Give me five!' shouted Barry playfully.

Rhys ran to him and slapped his father's hand in the time-honoured American tradition, before toddling off to the corner of the sparsely furnished room, where a pile of toy trucks and cars awaited his attention.

Carmen was looking at Charly's feet but was lost in her own thoughts. One of her daughter's pink socks had fallen off. It was cold in the room and her delicate little feet would have been frozen in minutes. Carmen kept staring at it. She was thinking about that wonderful summer when Rhys was just twelve months old. Barry had wanted him to be a soccer star and play for England then and he couldn't wait to take him fishing and do all the things fathers do with their sons. She took Charly swimming on the hot weekends and they had planned a holiday in Spain. It was a simple and easy life. They had taken long walks in Epping forest and told Charly what flowers to pick. The summer had passed leisurely for all of them, doing ordinary things and just being together.

Carmen snapped herself out of her daydream. It was almost as if her subconscious had sent her a message. She did everything subconsciously these days. She was on auto-pilot. She went over to the sofa to put Charly's sock back on, but Barry was already helping her. She smiled sadly, kissed him on the cheek and absent-mindedly straightened her hair. Then she sat down again. For the first time in a long while Carmen felt secretly frightened.

There was a knock at the door and Barry showed Kraft in. The squat American, dressed in wide black trousers, a black polo-neck jumper and loose jacket, looked like a dodgy, second-hand car salesman dealing on an east London bombsite. Who would have thought that so many conventional doctors testified to the ability of his unexplainable skills. He had a good track record — 25 years of remarkable success reversing incurable diseases, helping the paralysed to walk and killing cancer cells. He had been a 21-year-old musician when he first laid on hands as a joke and cured his brother's headache.

The American medical establishment was impressed with his work and he had endorsements from the University of Texas Cancer Center and the North Carolina General Assembly. But at £200 for a fifteen-minute session the treatment did not come cheap.

'Let us hope my paranormal energy can help,' he said, stroking Rhys's hair. 'It's an intuitive skill, but I have had about 85 per cent success in treating cases after the doctors have given up.'

Barry and Carmen nodded and Barry could have kicked himself for agreeing with him. Kraft could have said anything and he would have agreed. That irritated him.

'I know my fee is a little expensive, but I'm the best

in the world. I'm one of a kind. I can't make guarantees, but I have a good track record.'

Barry nodded again – and could have kicked himself again. Kraft explained that the brain was a very complex piece of apparatus and he could only direct his healing energy to where he believed the disease cells to be and pray that this would work.

He gently laid first Charly and then lively Rhys down on the little green sofa. Then he placed his hands on their heads for three sessions each of fifteen minutes.

His light touch made Rhys instantly sleepy. Within minutes his eyes closed and he was breathing deeply as Kraft's hands breezed over his tiny, tracksuited body.

Carmen and Barry watched bemused.

'I've never seen Rhys so calm,' said Barry out loud.

In an effort to explain himself, Kraft quietly spoke about 'paranormal energy' but gave the impression of a man who had as much understanding of his extraordinary gift as Barry or Carmen.

Barry was optimistic but Carmen was sceptical. They both knew, however, that hope was all they had left: they were praying for a miracle.

The telephone rang. It was a reporter from the *Daily Express*.

'Yes, Mr Kraft's here now,' said Barry. 'Yes, I heard about his work on a satellite TV programme. From the second I saw it, I decided we just had to try him. My wife Carmen is a believer in the real world, but she will try anything too, if it helps. I'm always open to suggestions. If people tell me I'm wasting my time, I'd like to put them in my position.'

The reporter asked him what the doctors had said about his trip to Amsterdam to see a psychic healer.

'I can understand that the medical profession

doesn't want to give us false hope,' said Barry, 'but inevitably their realism means we have been given no hope whatsoever. We have just had to make our own.'

After the call, Barry returned to Carmen's side to watch Kraft glide his hands over their son's little frame. Barry felt this was a man doing a worthwhile job. There were no guarantees with any form of medicine. He would have paid as much seeing a specialist in America for conventional treatment, so in his mind, all he was doing was trying other avenues.

Kraft was very confident and muttered on about everything and nothing – his past, why he was in Amsterdam, the people he had cured. But he would go silent as he tuned in to Charly or Rhys. There seemed to be a definite power transfer. Charly was on her knees one minute trying to jump up, the next minute she would roll over and then get back on to her knees again. She hadn't done that for six months.

Barry and Carmen stood in the claustrophobic Amsterdam hotel room watching the faith-healer. Whether it was a conventional bone marrow transplant or the mysticism of psychic healing, Barry and Carmen didn't care. They would try anything. It didn't matter what it was or what it cost. If they knew it could save their children they would sell their house and everything they owned. Three days later they were back in England, praying that Kraft had worked a miracle. Sadly he hadn't.

8: Don't Look Back

Professor Hobbs sounded confident; but then, he had always had a positive attitude right from the start.

'Yes, Professor. Yes, I know. Yes, I'll talk to Carmen. Yes, I'll ring you back. Yes, thank you.'

Barry put the telephone down. The professor had talked him round about Rhys's second transplant. Now all he had to do was persuade Carmen that Rhys should go through it all again.

Dr Oakhill came on the telephone, pleased that they were rethinking. He had an unrelated donor, a mismatch that he was willing to use. A week later Carmen agreed.

On 16 July 1994, Barry flew to Tel Aviv. In the back of his mind was the thought that he would be spending the following three months in Bristol with Rhys as soon as he returned. At least he had a little time to prepare himself. He often felt Carmen never had that opportunity, being with the children all the time. But Carmen had insisted that he should go. It was another business trip. A computer error at the Hilton needed sorting out and he was taking a work colleague with him. While he was there Barry discovered that the rock band Aerosmith were playing live at an outdoor concert in the Israeli capital, so he arranged tickets.

They booked into the sprawling Hilton hotel on the edge of the sea and one night drank with the boys from Aerosmith who were also staying there. In the wee small hours, as he walked to his room after one glass of wine too many, his thoughts drifted to how it might have been if situations had been different. How he might have made it with a big band. But he wouldn't swap what he had now for anything. He was married to a wonderful woman and he had two beautiful children who loved him ... and needed him. He fell asleep on the bed fully clothed.

At first, watching the sunlight fighting its way through the gap in the heavy green curtains, he couldn't recall where he was. Then, as it came back to him, he leaped out of bed, feeling like he had when he was a small boy on the first day of the school holidays, or in the mornings at the Atherfield Bay holiday camp, knowing that a good time was beckoning. He threw open the curtains and looked down at the shimmering blue swimming pool, to the east out across the sea and to the west the sprawling, white-walled city that held the promise of a carefree day. But then he felt guilty. Suddenly he didn't want to be there any more. It was sunny outside, but it was raining in his heart. He had never felt so much blackness. He needed to be back with Carmen, Charly and Rhys. For the next 24 hours all he thought about was the flight home. His mind also wandered to his brother David and how supportive he had been over the last two years, allowing Barry time off work to care for Charly and Rhys and finding him jobs that paid a few more bob around the globe.

* * *

'Here we go again, Rhys!'

Barry lifted his son into the back of the car. It was a sweltering hot August morning and Carmen hurried about the kitchen filling the flask with hot tea for the trip. Mr Al Fayed's personal assistant, Alison Smith, had stepped in and arranged the accommodation in Bristol. Barry and Carmen wondered what they would do without their guardian angel.

They both felt it would be harder this time. Rhys would suffer more going through a second transplant. Little Charly wasn't well enough to make the trek to Bristol so cousin Julie and friends Peter and Paula were helping out. The family would be broken up. Rhys would miss Charly, and Barry and Carmen would have to be separated a lot of the time too.

A few days later, former Rolling Stone Bill Wyman's personal assistant Penny Thompson rang Barry on his mobile phone.

'Bill is very moved by your story,' she said. 'He would like to help out.' Barry was thrilled. A meeting was set up at Bill's glitzy London restaurant Sticky Fingers to sort out a charity fund-raising event for October. Barry and Carmen had set up the Daniels Charitable Trust but they were still unsure how they should launch it.

Then came more good news. Early one afternoon a taxi arrived at the hospital stuffed full of toys. They were a present for Rhys from a businessman named David Richards who had been following Barry and Carmen's story and wanted to help in any way he could.

Barry rang David, who ran a promotions company in Letchworth, Hertfordshire, and he came over to Bristol offering the Daniels Charitable Trust office space once it had been launched in October.

Everything was beginning to come together now for Barry. He felt they were a family with a cause and would one day be able to help others. There was another lucky break too. David had many friends connected with the music industry and soon they were pitching in to help too.

For the next few weeks, as doctors prepared Rhys for his second, history-making bone marrow transplant, Barry was in touch with Penny Thompson every other day. Now a video of his children's story was going to be made for screening at the Sticky Fingers party to make everyone, stars included, aware of why they were there.

An initial £250,000 target had been set by Barry and Carmen for the Trust. The money raised would go to build and equip a transition house for eight to ten families whose children were being treated in Bristol Hospital far away from home. Barry also wanted the mothers and fathers to receive practical and moral support. The planned 'transition house' would be home to parents while their children were in the hospital and for the families when the youngsters came out of isolation. It would be built as close to the Bristol unit as possible. But Barry knew it was a daunting task. He needed building materials, beds, air-conditioning units, lights, furniture, plumbing . . . the list was getting bigger and bigger.

Carmen glanced around the bedroom where she had been lying in Barry's arms before he left to go to the little sealed isolation unit to see their son. She thought how unlived-in it felt, just like the rest of the flat really. The shadows of the morning were moving about, inching across the floor and then disappearing like little pools of black water that were suddenly sucked up by some invisible vacuum cleaner. She wondered if the transplant would really work this time. This was it, she knew that. There would be no third time.

The year had produced its own crop of problems, none of them as devastating as Batten's disease but sufficient enough to make her and Barry more than usually snappy, both at home and at the hospital. Money was always a worry and she hated having to rely on everyone's kindness and generosity when it came to equipment and help for her children.

It was indeed a beautiful day. The light had a sort of crystalline quality. She idly watched the bits of dust swirling around, caught in the ray of sunshine from the window, lots of specks, like little dots, like cells and enzymes and sugars and proteins and . . . she got up not wanting to think any more.

The effects of the second transplant together with a new batch of drugs were taking their toll on Rhys. He began to push away his oral tablets and became unsettled and miserable. His mouth was sore and his lips hurt. The doctor prescribed a low dose of Diamorphine and it seemed to help. But Carmen wasn't happy. It was the drug doctors put many cancer patients on when there was little hope. Now Rhys seemed like a four-year-old drug addict. He had bags under his eyes and his face was puffy. His eyeballs seemed to roll up under his eyelids. Carmen could hardly bare to watch. But she knew he had to have the drug – it was the only thing that would combat the terrible pain.

'Poor Rhys, you're not a happy chappy now,' said Barry one morning, trying to coax him into taking more tablets as Carmen entered the little cubicle.

Rhys slept and woke and tried to play with them,

then slept and woke and tried to play again. Carmen didn't think she could take much more. Once, as Rhys was sleeping, Barry took her in his arms and it was more than she could bear. She buried her face in his shoulder and sobbed without control. She was still crying when the nurse came in.

On the fifth day after the transplant Rhys seemed stronger. He asked for a jam sandwich – and then took two bites of it. Then he wanted sausages and he ate two, even though his lips were stinging.

On the sixth day though, things took a turn for the worse. He looked poorly after a rough night. His throat was burning and he struggled to swallow his tablets. He got up but made a little puddle on the floor.

Barry was distressed at seeing his son this way. Carmen had gone back home to Charly, but he needed to talk to her.

'I think he needs us both here,' he said over the telephone. 'He's so poorly.'

When he put down the phone he regretted his words. He had got upset and now he had upset Carmen. That wasn't what he had wanted to do. Damn it! He took a deep breath and rang her back, remembering the card she had left him on the bedroom table that morning before leaving.

A verse on the front read:

When I first met you, I knew there was something wonderful in store for me.

Now after all these years of being married to you, I know just how right I really was.

Every day with you has meant deepening love and understanding, celebrating the good things, facing what is hard, knowing that our love is stronger than any difficulty.

After all these years, my heart still soars when I am with you, and I find it hard to believe I could ever love someone so much . . . but I do.

You are my life.

Barry had put the card down as tears began to well up in his eyes. Then he picked it up again. Inside it read:

Dear Barry,

Just wanted you to know how much I love you and miss you.

As you say, things are hard sometimes but we know only too well that we have to get on with it.

You and our beautiful children are the most important things in the world to me and I love you all so much. It is very hard leaving you and Rhys behind, but I know that Charly needs just as much love as you two. I only wish I could split myself in two!

Love you deeply. See you Friday. Carmen xxx.

Barry's thoughts were broken when nurse Dawn came in at 4.30 p.m. and hooked Rhys up to his cardiac monitor before giving him more intravenous drugs. Rhys was distressed and sat on Barry's lap for two hours while the drug Phenytoin was pumped into him. Then he needed more vitamin K because his blood clotting wasn't right – a normal reaction to a bone marrow transplant. Barry finally left at around 8.00 that evening as Rhys fell into a deep sleep.

The next day was bad too. When Barry arrived he found Rhys sitting in the chair half asleep. His mouth was bad again and his throat. He had a high temperature and was very poorly. He put out his hands to his father, but they dropped down again because he didn't have enough strength. He couldn't open his mouth to say hello — he could only open it wide enough to spit out his saliva and have a little sob.

At 8 a.m. Carmen arrived and Rhys's face lit up — along with Barry's. There were lots of hugs and cuddles.

By now Rhys was on every conceivable drug, or so it seemed to Barry. When would they bring him back up? His eyes looked so droopy and his hair was coming out in handfuls. Barry took comfort in the fact that his son had picked up a lump of playdough and thrown it at him around 4 p.m.

The doctors were in stitches as they stood in the little sealed unit. It was Tuesday, 30 August, eleven days after the transplant and Rhys had left his hospital bed to play with some books and toys. But he obviously had an individual way of painting a picture. He got into a temper because the paint wouldn't go where he wanted it to on the paper. So he threw the pot in the air, and it landed on his head. Blue paint ran all over him. Everyone fell about laughing as Rhys sat pouting. But it wasn't long before his face broke into a cheeky grin as he realised everyone was watching.

His smile touched Barry and Carmen's hearts because his throat and mouth had been so sore since the surgery that he hadn't been able to laugh or talk. Even his frustration and the temper tantrums were signs of recovery. He seemed to be pulling through the worst now. Despite all the pain, he had got his sense of humour back. His white blood cell count was building up and the number of painkillers he was taking was going down.

Barry thanked Pete Waterman for his help. It was like the old days. He was back in a recording studio.

Multi-millionaire record producer Pete had lent Barry his Hit Factory studios in south-east London and a technical team to help out. Barry gazed around his office: the walls were adorned with pictures of old steam trains and railway plaques. It looked more like a miniature railway museum. Pete's love of trains had led him to buy the *Flying Scotsman*, the legendary engine from the age of steam. But that wasn't his only interest: he loved Koi carp too – and had bought a house in Japan, complete with a huge pond to keep his pet fish in.

The reception area of the building was crammed full of gold and platinum discs commemorating the huge success of the Waterman empire. Barry felt at home when he put on the earphones in the studio. He was recording in the studios where Kylie Minogue, Rick Astley and Bananarama had launched their careers, so he hoped some of the Waterman magic would rub off. Carmen was with Rhys in Bristol while he was cutting the track to run with the video for the charity launch at Sticky Fingers. He had to get back to Rhys's side so that Carmen could return to Charly.

The song was called 'Don't Look Back' and was co-written with his friend John Hociej, whom he believed had a wealth of musical talent. It was a powerful ballad built on Barry's faith, hope and fears. The first line summed up his emotions: 'Give me strength when there's no light to guide me, encouragement this comfort provides me.'

Barry had met John through the want-ads in a music magazine. John was advertising for a collaborator to work on new material and Barry rang him hoping that maybe this would be the chance to get back into his music and help release some of those pent-up emotions. As John only lived just down the road the arrangement was perfect. John had an eight-track home recording studio which offered great writing and demo-recording opportunities.

David Richards's friends became closely involved in the recording and the video for 'Don't Look Back'. Artist Julian Grater, whose works were very moving, was brought in and one of his paintings called *I Will Rise* was donated for the front cover of the record.

Later that month, Barry and Carmen's friends Susie Klee and Janet Sleppy arrived from America. Susie was fully aware of what they were going through as a family. For she had lost her daughter, Julie, at the age of ten to late infantile Batten's disease. They only stayed a couple of days but they all had so much to share and they were all praying for Rhys. Barry and Carmen enjoyed their company so much they wished they could stay.

Rhys finally left his isolation cubicle on 22 September and Britain was watching. The cameras clicked as he took his first wobbly steps in the open air after seven weeks sealed away from the world. He walked into the sunshine holding Barry's hand and wearing a tracksuit given to him by his favourite soccer team Tottenham Hotspur and his familiar baseball cap. Carmen, pushing Charly in her special buggy, followed close behind.

'We're moving into our flat nearby so that Rhys can have twice-daily check-ups at the hospital,' Barry told reporters. 'He's got lots of guts. He just wants to do what other boys his age do — run around and kick a football. He tries all the time. He loves the tracksuit from the Spurs squad, that was really kind of them. They've shown a lot of interest in Rhys and I'm grateful to them. Who knows — in fifteen years he might be up front knocking 'em in at White Hart Lane.'

Carmen stood quietly in the background wondering what the next 100 days would bring. That was the milestone they had to face now. The medical deadline was up at the end of November. Only then would they know whether the transplant was beginning to work.

The next day a very special little girl entered Rhys's old isolation cubicle. She was seven-year-old Nicola Swayles from Plymouth.

Barry and Carmen had been contacted by Nicola's family a few months earlier. She had been diagnosed as having juvenile Batten's disease and was pre-symptomatic. Her mother and father had been following the press coverage of Rhys and wanted to take a chance to save their daughter with a transplant. Barry and Carmen gave the family all the support they could, sharing the story of their ups and downs, heartache, joy and despair. It was, after all, a giant step for the Swayles to take.

On 23 September the transplant on Nicola went ahead and the work of the Daniels Charitable Trust was under way. The family could not find any accommodation to stay with their daughter in Bristol, so the Trust rented a flat that was suitable for them near the hospital. For Nicola would need all the support she could get from her immediate family in a safe haven for the after-care and specialist treatment, once the transplant was done and she was allowed out of isolation.

Barry and Carmen felt it was a tremendous achievement being able to make life a little easier for a family going through major stress, just like they were. At last they were doing something positive to help others.

183

Today Nicola is continuing her battle against the disease and the two families keep close links.

A few weeks later Barry, Carmen and Rhys were invited to meet Bill Wyman and model-turned-actress Paula Hamilton for a press call at Sticky Fingers. Charly wasn't well enough to go.

The TV and press cameras were again out in strength. It was the pre-photo session for the charity launch party at Sticky Fingers on 27 October. Rhys took to Bill straight away and the ex-Rolling Stone was clearly in his element.

Carmen woke up and looked at the alarm clock. It was 5 a.m. and it was the day she had been dreading for weeks – video day, the day for making the tape for 'Don't Look Back' that would accompany the big charity launch. It was being shot by Oyster Productions, which had been brought in by Mike Loveday, a friend of David Richards, who had been a great help in putting the project together. Everyone involved wanted the video to be as true to life as possible. Carmen and Barry had been told to play their parts – but Carmen's was the biggest role.

At 6.30 a.m. TV crews, vans, lighting, lorries, the works arrived on the front doorstep. It was hard to keep it all quiet as the camera rigs rolled behind Carmen walking down Epping High Street, kicking leaves in a churchyard and strolling through the park. The cameras caught the moment wonderfully, with Rhys cuddling and kissing Charly and Barry and Carmen hugging each other, their faces lost in thought. The video also included pictures of Rhys lying in his hospital bed with no hair during the first transplant and Charly being carried in her mother's arms as Barry's voice could be heard singing 'Don't

Look Back'. The children's playground scenes were shot with the help of youngsters from St John's Primary School and many of Barry and Carmen's cousins and friends.

At 7 p.m. it was finished. The end of a full day. Carmen, Barry, Charly and Rhys were exhausted. The next morning Barry was back at the Hit Factory putting the finishing touches to 'Don't Look Back'. There were day and night sessions until it was finally completed.

The story video and the recording were great, but there was something missing. Barry felt he had to appeal to a younger audience. He approached another production company, Caplan and Wilkie, in his search for an alternative mix. Time was running out: there was only a week to the launch.

A young director named Paul Harper set up the shoot with VMTV at the Molinare studios in London's Carnaby Street. The video was remade and the original artwork for the cassette and CD, featuring the painting *I Will Rise* by Julian Grater, was also filmed as a backdrop for the five-minute clip. The result of the complete project, audio and visual, was very moving. Barry believed it was a great accomplishment.

All in all things were on an even keel now. Rhys seemed to be getting stronger every day, although he sometimes got tired and irritable. Charly was still eating well, probably better than many other children of her age. She loved meat and two veg and sausages, egg and chips and Sunday roast. Her fluid intake was the only worry: she just would not finish her water or orange or vitamin drinks. Barry and Carmen persevered trying to get her to swallow from a cup almost every hour. They didn't know what the next day would bring.

* * *

The launch party at Sticky Fingers was a huge success. The stars were quick to come out and sparkle for Rhys. Paula Hamilton looked daring in a Versace gown, athlete Linford Christie laughed and joked with singer Lisa B and Valerie Campbell, supermodel mum of Naomi Campbell, did her bit modelling clothes donated for auction by other famous names. The highlight was a wedding dress worn over thigh-high boots. The whole thing was hosted by Russ Kane of London's Capital Radio and Barry and Carmen's friend, Channel 4's *Big Breakfast* presenter Gaby Roslin.

Many of the TV, film and stage celebrities sat with tears in their eyes as they watched the 'Don't Look Back' video. The words scrolled up in front of them:

The Daniels Charitable Trust has been set up to help families who like the Daniels have to travel and live for prolonged periods of time away from home while caring for a seriously sick child.

By providing practical, financial and moral support, the Trust hopes to ease some of the enormous stress which afflicts so many families in similar circumstances each year.

Please help the Daniels Charitable Trust to make life a little easier for those families who need it most.

Bill Wyman told pressmen later: 'And I think I'm having problems when my baby doesn't sleep at night.

'Barry and Carmen haven't just had one huge problem, they have had two. But with all that going on they are still trying to help other kids. I think that is fantastic.'

During the evening there were live performances by Phil Cool, Justin Hayward, formerly of the sixties band The Moody Blues and Peter Cunnah of the pop group D:Ream. A major highlight was a painting of Rhys donated by the artist known as Trademark. Bill Wyman finally outbid everyone at £15,000, but the previous bidder, the former Hard Rock Café owner Barry Cox, still donated his £14,000 offer to the charity, making the total for the painting £29,000. Everyone that night had a heart of gold. More than £45,000 had been raised by the time Bill took to the stage with his wife Suzanne and made a special announcement.

'Suzanne and I would like Barry and Carmen to have this wonderful painting of their son Rhys,' he said.

Barry and Carmen were stunned. What a fabulous evening. The Trust had got off to a great start. Now it could help families just like Mohamed Al Fayed had helped them. In his heart Barry didn't know what they would have done without him.

It was a cold November afternoon when Barry, Carmen and Charly arrived at Great Ormond Street. They were used to hospitals now, the crowded car parks, the busy corridors, the slow lifts, stretchers on wheels stuck in corners and endless rows of people sitting on endless rows of red plastic seats in long corridors lined with cheap paintings and waiting for their names to be called.

Mr Al Fayed, the Harrods chairman, had arranged for them to see Dr Ricky Richardson when he learned that they had been upset with the lack of follow-through on Charly from Great Ormond Street. There were so many things Barry and Carmen had not been made aware of that could have made her little life more comfortable.

Charly was now in leg-splints and that presented a whole series of new problems they had never expected. If only they had known what to expect.

They were met at the hospital by Ruth Williams from University College Hospital and Professor Gardiner's team who were working on mapping the chromosome for the defective gene that caused Charly's illness. More blood samples were taken and Dr Richardson arranged for a full physio assessment. Due to Charly's lack of movement, one of her hips appeared to be becoming dislocated. If it did, she would suffer tremendously.

It was obvious that Charly needed more physio work and a hydrotherapy or Jacuzzi bath at home. Barry and Carmen knew how expensive that could be. But they would get it somehow.

David Richards's secretary Lisa used to work for Jacuzzi in the UK and that provided the breakthrough Barry needed. She rang her contacts and explained about Charly's condition. Within a week a Jacuzzi was on its way. Meanwhile back in Epping Jackie and Keith Davis set up another fund-raising event – The Bath Appeal. Money still had to be found to refit the bathroom to take the bath and other bits of equipment. A few weeks later the Jacuzzi arrived and it was like a whale. Barry couldn't believe how big it was when he saw it on the drive. Now he had to get it up the stairs. He and two neighbours turned it this way and that, putting it upside down and sideways until they could squeeze it in the front door. They puffed and blew, tugged and pushed and pulled. Finally, they got it into the bathroom. Days later Charly's little tired legs were being massaged in jets of water in her home. Barry and Carmen wondered how much pain their daughter would have been in but for that latest visit to Great Ormond Street, courtesy of Mr Al Fayed.

Barry and Carmen hugged each other in the lounge, unable to let the other go. The telephone call was the best news ever. Rhys's hundred days transplant tests were fine. The marrow was showing signs of engrafting strongly and new cells were continually growing. No problems. Last time the donor cells began to die away immediately. There had been only a small percentage left after the first 100 days. But it was still too early to carry out any tests for Batten's disease because the new marrow would take at least a year to engraft properly. It was crucial that the cells survived so that they could start to penetrate the blood–brain barrier and work on the affected cells in the brain – the centre of the terrible disease. It was a tough job for the cells. As Barry had been told, the blood–brain barrier was like the Pentagon – unless you've got a pass it was sometimes impossible to get in.

'Let's have some wine,' said Barry, and Carmen nodded, quietly, still afraid. He looked at her knowing her thoughts. 'Come on, we'll take each day as it comes, as we always do.'

Barry stood in the new charity offices at the Pixmore Centre in Letchworth, Hertfordshire, donated to the Trust by David Richards. The BBC were arriving any minute to do a news feature on the Trust. Barry stared out of the window, down at the car park: it had been a long, hard, sad road to get here, he thought. But it was a great feeling to see the charity growing into a tree from a small seed.

By now things were under way for the Variety Club

of Great Britain's Gold Heart Day, scheduled for 14 February.

The annual four-week appeal had raised more than £14 million to help sick, disabled and disadvantaged children in the United Kingdom since it had been launched in 1991. Each tiny Gold Heart brooch, sold nationwide for £1, was a symbol of love, care and the Variety Club's efforts to make life a little easier for youngsters in need. In the first year, more than a million Gold Hearts were bought; in 1992 more than three million people showed they cared. The third year had been better still and so too had the fourth. Now the Variety Club was aiming for £5 million to help finance a vast range of projects for the benefit of children. The brooches were sold at major stores such as W H Smiths, Boots, Mothercare, Little Chef and Index, the catalogue shop.

Barry met the Variety Club's international president John Ratcliffe and his wife Marsha for lunch in the Hertfordshire countryside and was at once overwhelmed by their honesty and caring. Marsha struck him as being almost angelic and a bit like royalty at the same time. He couldn't quite get over it. Could she really be for real?

Silver-haired John was a successful businessman. But now both he and Marsha went all over the world helping children in need. It was all in their own time and mostly at their own expense. They told him so many stories about children in need that he felt comforted in a strange kind of way.

They were both very moved by the story of Charly and Rhys and promised to help in any way they could, inviting Barry to join the Gold Heart campaign. He readily agreed.

Barry left thrilled to be working hand in hand with

one of the greatest children's charities in the world. The plan was for him to appear with Carmen, Charly and Rhys on the Sky TV telethon on St Valentine's Day for a live interview. An extract from the 'Don't Look Back' video would be played. The telethon, the climax of the campaign, was the brainchild of ever-smiling Variety Club crew member Raymond Curtis, himself a successful businessman, and Sky TV producer Martin Fox.

9: Our Prince Among Royals

The occasion was too much for Rhys. Sometimes being brave just wasn't enough to stop the tears rolling. All the emotion of the awards ceremony overwhelmed him – and not even a royal touch could comfort him. The Duchess of Kent, whose hugs had been known to make even Wimbledon losers feel better, had presented Rhys with a Children of Courage award. Moments later he broke down in tears.

It was 18 December 1994, at Westminster Abbey. Barry and Carmen and Rhys had spent the night before the ceremony, sponsored by *Woman's Own* magazine, at the St Ermin's hotel, not far from the Abbey.

They were worried that the commotion at the event would be too much for Charly and so they had left her with cousin Julie at home. They were also worried about Rhys being affected by the hustle and bustle of the ceremony so soon after his second transplant, but the magazine executives assured them that they would be free to do whatever they felt necessary if Rhys wasn't up to all the party arrangements. It was a hectic schedule.

Barry and Carmen settled into a suite at the hotel, which had been beautifully decorated for Christmas. Rhys had been more interested in the huge Christmas tree in the front lobby than all the people saying hello to him.

'Christmas trees have always fascinated him,' Barry told the doorman. 'He loves colourful things like decorations and pretty, fairytale lights.'

'I did too when I was his age . . . a long time ago,' the doorman replied.

'It was a long time ago for me too,' said Barry.

'Longer for you than for me,' joked Carmen.

They both smiled and the doorman did too.

Barry and Carmen and Rhys met some of the other families whose children were receiving awards at dinner that evening but went to bed early to save their energy for the glittering events the following day.

That night Barry and Carmen sat talking and looking back at what Rhys had been through over the past two years, his pioneering transplant and all the traumas associated with it.

'Remember the donor search?' asked Carmen.

'And that ethical review we thought would go on and on?' replied Barry.

'How will I ever forget it . . . and that bloody closure of the Westminster Hospital.'

They talked about the court case that followed and reflected on the press coverage and having to put Rhys through a high-risk second transplant. Then they remembered the horrific side effects of the chemotherapy and immuno-suppressant drugs that Rhys had suffered.

'You know what I think about this award, Carmen?'

'No, what?'

'Well, I think Rhys has earned it . . . but not just for himself. For his big sister too.'

Carmen could hardly bring herself to answer. They lay in silence for a while. Then she said: 'In a way I think Rhys knows that too.'

They both lay silent now, thinking. They knew that Charly had suffered the worst effects of Batten's disease and if it hadn't been for her they wouldn't have got an early diagnosis on Rhys, and he would never have had the chance to start his battle for life.

'Baz.'

'Yes?'

'I love you.'

'I love you too, Carmen. No one can take that away from us.'

The next morning a crowd of photographers and reporters saw the special bus off outside the hotel and Rhys waved to them through the window. He waved again to the press as they arrived with the other families at the Abbey. He was the youngest of all the children being honoured and he was a bit bewildered by it all.

Inside the wonderful old building where so many royals had been married, Barry, Carmen and Rhys were escorted to the front row. The seats in the Abbey were nearly full and as they sat down someone called: 'Barry, Barry!'

It was Bill Wyman and his wife Suzanne sitting a few rows back. Rhys waved at them too, and every few minutes during the music he would ask: 'Where's Bill? I want to see Bill.'

'OK, Rhys, we'll see Bill when we've seen the Duchess,' said Barry.

Now Rhys was completely baffled. He hadn't heard the word 'duchess' before.

Barry marvelled at all the other plucky youngsters at the London ceremony. He watched as the Duchess of Kent spoke to soccer-mad Dale Jones who had arrived from Nottinghamshire. Eight-year-old Dale's foot had had to be amputated when he suffered the brain disease meningitis but he refused to let the handicap keep him from playing. He had been fitted with an artificial foot and still turned out for his school football team. His hero, Southampton skipper Matthew Le Tissier, was at the awards to congratulate Dale on his bravery and present him with a signed football.

Barry's eyes watered when he heard the story of Robbie Cowin from the Isle of Man. The five-year-old had been terribly burnt on his back and head after falling into a scalding bath. For the first four months of his treatment he could only sleep balanced on his knees and forehead. But little Robbie was less worried by the pain than losing his red hair. Now his worries were over. Pioneering surgery had restored a healthy scalp and he had his carroty locks back. They were all such plucky kids.

When Rhys's turn came, actor Anthony Andrews introduced his story and then invited him up on the stage. The Duchess of Kent presented him with the award and offered words of encouragement and admiration for his spirit. She also told Barry and Carmen how concerned she was for them as parents. Barry was quite choked up for a few seconds. It was such a proud moment.

After the ceremony they all went into a reception room in the back of the Abbey, where they mingled with the celebrities from the world of pop, stage and TV who had come to support the children, and Rhys finally got to give Bill a cuddle. Somehow a bond was growing between them.

Then came the photo call. Rhys had been OK so far, but he was getting tired. It was his first big outing since the transplant. Everyone walked back into the Abbey and the photographers and TV news crews were wall to wall.

The children gathered together around the Duchess and the lights started flashing, which seemed to upset Rhys and he began to get grumpy and cried. The Duchess tried to cheer him up, but it wasn't working.

'Baz, I think he's having a seizure,' said Carmen.

'Better get him,' said Barry.

They walked over and plucked him away, making their apologies. But everyone seemed to apologise to them. What a funny old world.

Ever since Rhys's second transplant some of the after-care drugs had made him susceptible to mild fits. Now the big occasion was all too much for him and Barry and Carmen took him back to the hotel.

Rhys slept for a couple of hours and when he woke up he was in a better mood.

'Let's go walkabout,' said Barry.

Rhys laughed and clapped at the soldiers on Horse Guards Parade. Barry pretended to knock on the door of Buckingham Palace for afternoon tea and then told Rhys the Queen was out.

Back at the hotel there were sacks of presents for the children – and *Woman's Own* gave Carmen a bag of gifts for Charly. She and Barry were very moved. Rhys spent the whole of the afternoon tea session showing off his medal and scroll signed by his new friend, the Duchess. From that day on, Barry always touched the medal for good luck. And somehow it seemed to work.

That evening at home Barry and Carmen were

tired but didn't want to go to bed. They sat with Charly for a while and when she was asleep went into the lounge to read all the letters of comfort they had received from well-wishers as they had done so many times. Barry put some of them in his files and by chance came across the diagnosis sheets from the Batten's disease clinic in New York. It all seemed such a long time ago.

He looked at the headings. They were all so clinical:

CLIENT: Daniels, Rhys. AGE: 15 months. SEX: Male. COLLECTED: October 1993.

Barry understood the words more now than he had done at that time and he sat reading them silently to himself:

This ultrastructural lymphocyte study showed numerous cells containing lysosomes filled with curvilinear bodies and islands of electron dense profiles.

Diagnostic impression: late infantile neuronal ceroid. Four one-micron slides and three ultrastructure grids were examined for this study.

Charly's diagnosis sheet read more or less the same which Barry found suddenly depressing.

He picked up the histopathology report that had been produced at Great Ormond Street in February 1992.

Another clinical heading:

SURNAME: Daniels. FORENAMES: Charlotte. SEX: Female. HOSPITAL NUMBER: 9109886. LOCATION: Ward ICD. CONSULTANT; Wilson, Dr. J.

Again he read it to himself:

Microscopy shows cryostat sections with large bowel mucosa, submucosa and some circular muscle coat. The changes are those of Batten's disease and are indicative of the late infantile form. Electron microscopy for confirmation will follow.

There was also a press release from the Batten's Disease Institute in America that had gone all over the world. It told the Daniels' story . . .

With the court battle behind them, this family faced both hope and despair. A bone marrow transplant has never been performed on a Batten's disease patient. But, if they were to stop the disease before the onset of the symptoms, the bone marrow transplant was their only hope. What if it didn't stop the disease? What if his body rejected the new bone marrow? There were many what ifs. The alternative was to let their son die. This courageous couple felt that Rhys's only chance for a normal life was to go ahead with the transplant and pray to God it would work.

Barry fell asleep.

On 16 January Barry and Carmen took Rhys to the Gold Heart campaign launch at the Park Lane Hilton in London. Charly was too ill to go. She was having problems eating. Carmen was distraught that she was not having enough fluids. But they had to put on a brave face. Hours before they left for the event they both sat either side of their daughter cradling her in their arms.

Charly was screaming and crying with pain.

'I can't go. I can't go,' said Carmen.

'OK, OK, we'll both stay with Charly,' said Barry. He desperately wanted to climb inside his daughter's mind and destroy whatever was hurting her.

As time passed Charly settled down and the pain subsided. They waited for a while and when everything seemed all right decided to chance it.

The occasion was filmed live for the BBC's Pebble Mill and Gloria Hunniford compered the show. Barry, Carmen and Rhys shared a table with *Lovejoy* star Ian McShane and his wife Gwen who had been following their story in the newspapers. And there were lots of hugs from Julia Morley.

Carmen was talking but not talking. Everyone seemed to understand what she and Barry were going through. But they weren't living it. Her mind was constantly on Charly.

By now Charly was having real problems with her eating and she and Barry were distressed. Charly wasn't getting enough fluids and was experiencing problems with a dry mouth and dry skin. Barry was deeply upset holding his daughter in his arms as she screamed and cried with pain. She couldn't tell him why she hurt because she couldn't talk any more. Her sobs cut him like a knife. He was her father, he should be making the pain go away and he couldn't. As he sat with Rhys at the Variety Club event his mind was elsewhere. There must be something he could do, but what? That day both he and Carmen desperately needed to get home, to find an answer.

The next morning they called Charly's local neurologist. But he was on holiday. They called Great Ormond Street – but no appointments were available. They called Dr Ricky Richardson and left a message. An hour or so later he called back.

Dr Richardson talked them through their options. He was like a voice from heaven. By the time Barry put down the telephone he felt much better. Days later the local community nurse came to the house and fitted a nasal gastric tube to Charly for feeding. Charly hated it and she cried in pain. Barry and Carmen tried to reassure her.

'I want to bloody well rip it out, Carmen!'

'I know, I know, but we can't. We have to try and get on top of this feeding problem quickly. It's the best way.'

Barry was finally convinced. Well, almost. Finally, he arranged an emergency appointment at Great Ormond Street where a gastrostomy was fitted. This meant Charly having a tube inserted directly through her stomach wall, which was operated by a shut-off valve. Now she could be tube-fed regularly without too much of a problem. Soon she seemed to settle down, and could still take some food by mouth, but very little. It seemed as if Charly was fading away in front of Barry's eyes.

And, to make matters worse, Rhys seemed unstable on his feet. Could it be the cocktail of drugs he was still taking following the transplant?

At Great Ormond Street Hospital, Dr Wilson was pleased with Rhys's progress, but he felt that he should be taken off the drug Phenytoin because it could cause ataxia in some children. Barry and Carmen began to wean their little son off the drug that same night.

During the following few weeks, Rhys, still on a mild dose of Phenytoin, lost all use of his legs. He couldn't stand properly or even take one step. Barry and Carmen were distraught. They believed it was the beginning of the end.

They sat one morning at the kitchen table staring out at the sleet flicking at the window and running down in little narrow rivers to the sill. They were both resigned now. So much had been thrown at them over the last few years that they just accepted anything bad that came their way. Carmen remembered how Charly had bumped into things and stumbled and fallen down the slides in the park. They talked a lot about Charly, about how pretty she was and the modelling sessions and the visits to Disneyworld. The memories were recalled one by one, as they are in all families. But all the time in the back of their minds was Rhys, his stumbling and not being able to walk properly. He had to be carried everywhere now or taken out in a special pushchair.

Carmen had always suffered from backache from carrying Charly, but it was twice as bad now that she had to pick her son up all the time too.

The stars were out in force and it was a night Barry and Carmen would never forget – the Variety Club of Britain's Gold Heart Day.

It was a cold, windy and wet afternoon when they arrived outside the London Television Centre on the south bank of the Thames. They were lucky enough to find a parking spot near the building and were luckier still to see Carmen's father Brian, his wife Marianne and her brother Steven walking towards them. They all helped unload the car and carry Charly and Rhys into the studios.

Rhys loved the huge, almost empty room they were escorted into and he managed to totter about for a while without getting in anyone's way, before Carmen picked him up and put him back in the pushchair. Producers, cameramen and programme executives seemed to be rushing around too, tearing their hair out as the countdown to the 6.00 p.m. start of the telethon drew near. Barry wondered whether it would all come together.

There was a live link-up with the *Daily Express* over at London's Blackfriars Bridge where a junior newsroom had been set up. A group of children, some of them disabled, would be following the telethon and creating pages for the newspaper on the story of the show, which included dance-athons, hair-athons, and basketball-athons live from Wembley.

Barry and Carmen were called down to the studio at around 6.30 p.m. There were famous faces everywhere. The pop group Let Loose was waiting to perform, actress Britt Ekland was standing in the wings, Status Quo were milling around, John and Marsha Ratcliffe of the Variety Club were on hand and then in walked Bill Wyman, who was playing later that evening.

In the glittering, star-studded marathon of fundraising events around the country from Wembley to Scotland and Bournemouth to Dublin, dozens of celebrities were giving their services to boost the appeal.

Scores of people, some of them actors and singers, were manning the telephone lines, taking cash pledges from thousands of caring callers. In return Valentine messages to their loved ones would be flashed across the screen.

'It's so wonderful to be part of all this,' Carmen said to Barry.

'Come on, we're on,' he replied.

'Barry!'

'What?'

'Look at Chris Tarrant.'

'Why?'

'I just can't believe how tall he is.'

Barry didn't have time to look at the TV presenter because minutes later they were in front of the cameras telling the story of their struggle to beat Batten's disease to Anna Walker. She was so moved she had to wipe a tear from her eye before she could continue. Barry's song 'Don't Look Back' was played at the end of the interview and the audience seemed very moved too.

Carmen was very affected by Anna.

'What a pretty lady, the camera doesn't do her justice. I just felt she was so nice, so genuine,' she said to Barry as they left the set.

Rhys was suddenly mesmerised. He couldn't believe that he had bumped into Saracen from the TV show *Gladiators*. They quickly became friends.

'Rhys loves your show,' said Barry. 'He mimics all you gladiators with an inflatable hammer, jumping around the soft room we've built for him at home. Sorry though, Wolfman is his favourite.' They all laughed.

Later they sat talking to Bill and Suzanne Wyman about Charly and Rhys. Bill too got visibly upset as he learned more about the disease. Barry realised then just how sensitive the ex-Rolling Stone was about life.

Barry and Carmen stayed for a while soaking up the electrifying atmosphere, sometimes in awe of how many famous people they saw. They watched Bill and his band do their set with Georgie Fame and then they left because Charly was tired.

Brian and Marianne took Charly and Rhys home with them – planning the route to take in a McDonald's drive-in for Rhys who was hungry again. He had a craze now for chicken nuggets.

Then Barry and Carmen headed for Sticky Fingers where a special party was being thrown by Bill. All their friends were there, among them Pete, Trish,

Julie, Peter and Paula, Jacky and Keith, Karen and Steven. And more stars . . . actor Steve Thompkinson of the TV show *Drop the Dead Donkey*, the *Sun* newspaper's page-three beauty Suzie Mittzi, some of the boys from pop group Spandau Ballet, and many more.

It was a night Barry and Carmen would never forget. They were treated like stars too and given three tables for their friends where they were toasted with champagne. Barry and Carmen hadn't laughed so much for years.

A few hours later it was all over. Time to go home. Carmen felt like Cinderella at the ball. She had to leave for her other world again. For the first time in a long time, she had felt like a person again.

The following week Charly went into Great Ormond Street for day surgery. All went well, and there didn't seem to be any complications. But the doctor wanted to keep her in overnight for observation. Carmen was adamant. She refused. She had seen her children in hospital too often.

'She'll be much more comfortable in her own bed,' she insisted. The doctors relented.

Barry and Carmen took their daughter home. She was being tube-fed now with a special vitamin formula and lots of fluids. She was still eating, but only sometimes, when she felt like it.

That night they lay in bed talking about what one doctor had told them. He said that tube-feeding Charly would only prolong the agony and in that case they would all have to suffer for a few more years.

'Who cares if we suffer,' said Carmen. 'She is our daughter and her being comfortable is more important. I mean, who could starve their child to death?

That's what we would be doing if we didn't tube-feed her.'

'I know.' said Barry. 'Every minute with her is priceless. I wonder how the doctor would feel in our position?'

They both lay silent for a while. Then Charly began to cry. It was the best sound in the world. One day they knew they wouldn't hear her crying any more.

There was laughter in the living room. Carmen liked that. She wanted everyone to have fun. She wanted to hear the sound of people enjoying themselves. Her and Barry's friends Peter and Paula were round, drinking beer and eating sandwiches and talking about music and politics and doing the kind of things friends do.

Peter and Paula's daughter, also named Charly, was romping on the floor with Rhys and urging him to get up and dance with her as Carmen brought in some more coffee.

Suddenly, everyone went quiet. Rhys had stood up and was now running around the room. He hadn't been able to walk for months.

Barry and Carmen shouted to each other to watch. They just couldn't believe it. Then the penny dropped. Rhys's Phenytoin was at a record low. It must have been the drug after all. Carmen almost cried as Barry swept Rhys up in his arms. From that moment on their little son went from strength to strength.

By 1 April 1995, Rhys was completely free of the drug Phenytoin and was even climbing the stairs by himself. It was hard for Barry and Carmen to believe that the drug could have had such an adverse effect on Rhys's balance and his ability to walk, but the proof was there for all to see. No one could deny it, not even Rhys's consultant in Bristol, Dr Colin Steward. He was amazed to see that just one drug could make such a difference.

Barry was motoring again. Now that Rhys was on the up and up he needed to head to America. There were more specialists to see, like Dr Michael Bennett at the Dallas Children's Hospital in Texas.

Dr Bennett had moved to America from England to further his research into Batten's disease. He was working with juvenile Batten's patients and according to reports there were some really promising signs that his treatments were helping. He had already agreed to look at Rhys's cultured skin cells and he wanted to try a course of fish oils on him. That would make Rhys the first late infantile patient to receive such a form of treatment.

After a nine-hour flight to Dallas's Fort Worth airport, Barry and Carmen and Charly and Rhys were welcomed by their American friends Susie and Janet. It had been Charly's seventh birthday the day before and they presented her with a beautiful birthday cake decorated in the shape of the state of Texas and, of course, a yellow rose.

It was a wonderful three days and Susie's husband Doug spent hours with Charly on his lap stroking her hair. Their daughter Julie had died on 25 February 1993, aged ten, another helpless victim of Batten's disease.

Barry burnt the midnight oil with Doug talking about his daughter Julie. It seemed as if they had a special bond as fathers fighting a long, hard battle. They had both experienced the despair of seeing the devastating disease destroy lives.

Three days later, Charly was too ill to travel on and Barry and Carmen were pleased that Susie and Doug had offered to look after her. Their other two children, Tyler and Paige, were pleased too.

Barry, Carmen and Rhys arrived in Florida just as the rain stopped. First port of call was Sea World and Shamu the killer whale. He was one of Rhys's favourites: he loved getting soaked when Shamu decided it was time to have a splash.

Then they went off to visit Rick and Linda in San Antonio. It was a great reunion. The next day Barry and Carmen visited Dr Thomas Dooley at the Department of Genetics, Southwest Foundation for Biomedical Research. Barry had talked to Tom in New York a few months earlier at the Batten's disease conference.

Tom gave him and Carmen a full-scale tour of his 200-acre research centre for molecular biology. It housed the largest colony of baboons in the world. Barry and Carmen were fascinated.

A few days later Rick gave a barbecue and he invited Tom and his wife and family over. It was a chance for Barry and Carmen to talk more to the man they had come to respect. They were hungry for knowledge. Strange, but just a few years earlier Tom and his wife had lived just up the road from Epping in Woodford, east London. Their daughter Jena was born only two months after Charly . . . and in the same hospital in Walthamstow. What a small world.

'Barry, I'm scared!'
    'Why?' Barry rolled over in bed.
    'The tornado.'
    There had been news flashes on television about the

tornado warning. Barry had heard it all before. He had experienced similar warnings in South Dakota as a hopeful rock star. In his mind it seemed a regular occurrence.

'It's just a twirler,' he said.

'What's a twirler?'

'It's something that rips your life apart . . . like the tornado of Batten's disease that has ripped our life apart.'

Behind the brick walls of two unprepossessing buildings in a science park at Rockville, Maryland, 135 scientists and entrepreneurs were laying the groundwork for a new tomorrow in biology and medicine. Computer-assisted robots, the galley slaves of the twenty-first century, were working around the clock in a spotless, brightly lit bay doing the researchers' bidding. The object was to decipher and commercialise the chemical sequences that make up human genes, the molecular arbiters of health, intelligence and behaviour.

The researchers, robots and computers were all part of Human Genome Sciences, the largest and the most lavishly financed of about a dozen new companies in America racing to crack the human genetic code.

The benefits would be enormous. Like Texas dirt farmers who became rich in the land rush by discovering oil on their property, the gene entrepreneurs were hoping to hit the jackpot too. And if they did, the rewards would be ginormous. But Humane Genome Sciences was only one of the organisations joining the genetic lottery.

Barry put down the magazine article. Carmen was asleep and her bedside light was on. He leant over and turned it off and lay peacefully in the still of the night.

He didn't care who made money. He just wanted them, anyone, to succeed in beating Batten's disease.

He knew that decoding the fundamental secrets of life would pay off. With genetic codes in hand, scientists would be able to design drugs to attack the causes of disease rather than the symptoms, as most medications did now. Afflictions that had crippled and killed for millenniums – cancers, rheumatoid arthritis, heart disease, cystic fibrosis and Batten's disease – could become curable. So would such smaller miseries as migraine headaches and obesity. Even baldness could be treatable.

'Who cares who makes the money,' Barry said under his breath before falling asleep.

Finally, the day came when they had to return home. Carmen vowed not to get upset and cry as she always did when saying farewell. Susie and Doug drove them to the airport where they were met by airline staff who took extra care of Charly and Rhys.

It was terribly hard for Susie and Doug to say goodbye to Charly, not knowing if they would ever see her again. Tears were flowing. Carmen couldn't even bring herself to speak. The plane took off and they were gone. As soon as the 757 touched down in London, Carmen was on the telephone to Dallas and Susie. The lines kept sizzling for weeks.

Barry picked up the telephone. It was another reporter.

'Yes, Rhys is going from strength to strength. Yes, he runs all over the house. No, our battle isn't over. We will never give up until this terrible disease is beaten and children throughout the world don't suffer any more. The strength that keeps us going is our ability to help other families in similar circumstances.

Anyone who joins our campaign to rid the earth of this disease becomes our friend. At the moment, we are only a small team but we will never give up hope or lose the faith we have in what we are doing or in each other.'

Barry put down the telephone and turned to Carmen.

'I wonder what will happen next, Baz,' she said.

He thought for a moment, then said: 'Whatever happens, we'll just take each day as it comes, like we always do.'

**THE DANIELS
CHARITABLE TRUST**
Registered Charity No. 1036041

'CARING FOR THE NEEDS OF FAMILIES AND THEIR SICK CHILDREN'

If you would like to know more about the work of the Daniels Charitable Trust, please write to us, enclosing a stamped addressed envelope, at:

>The Daniels Charitable Trust
>Pixmore Centre
>Pixmore Avenue
>Letchworth
>Hertfordshire SG6 1JG

Any donations for our work will be gratefully received.